*Church
Planting
at the End
of the
Twentieth
Century*

Charles L. Chaney

Church planting at the end of the twentieth century

Tyndale House Publishers, Inc.   *Wheaton, Illinois*

*To the Churches
of the
Illinois Baptist
State Association*

and

*To the Staff
of the Church
Extension Division
of IBSA*

*For whom
and with whom
the work of
the last nine years
has been
both joyful
and meaningful*

First printing, March 1982
Library of Congress Catalog Card Number 81-84602
ISBN 0-8423-0279-4, paper
Copyright © 1982 by Charles L. Chaney

Contents

Foreword

Church Planting in America is an exciting, convincing book about an urgent task confronting every congregation and every denomination. Chapter after chapter talks about real situations. "Yes" we say, "that is exactly how it is. Dr. Chaney is describing our churches and speaking to our real needs. He is asking the right questions and setting forth sensible answers. He has been there. He knows the field."

Readers will be struck by the enormous unchurched populations in the United States. In a typical city which Chaney uses as an illustration, if all the churches were to be filled to capacity—every seat occupied—less than half of the population of that city would have been to church.

Chaney points out that in most white denominations, and especially among their leadership, upper middle-class culture is dominant. If the lower middle classes and the laboring masses are to be churched, we must have a vast multiplication of congregations which fit *them,* in which *they* feel at home, where *they* are in charge.

This book on church planting in North America is helpful for other continents also. Its plea for congregations which fit every segment of humanity, every people, every economic and educational class must be heard in Asia, Africa, Europe, and Latin America.

Though Dr. Chaney has deliberately confined himself to
the United States, and though most of his illustrations
come from its seven central northern states, what he is
saying is directly applicable to the spread of the
Christian faith in all lands. Missionaries and national
church leaders everywhere can read this book with
great profit.

   Dr. Chaney speaks from the viewpoint of the vast
unchurched. For example, he says bluntly that the phrase
"declining transitional communities" is an expression
of white chauvinism. From the point of view of the
incoming multitudes, the transitional community is *not*
declining. It is a place of great promise — otherwise
people would never move there. Many other examples
could easily be given. If the lost are to be found, Christians
must go where the lost are, and church them in
congregations which are agreeable and pleasant and
uplifting *to them.* The Gentiles will be discipled by
Christians who eat ham. Jews will be discipled by those
who don't.

   The complex and difficult field of the transitional
communities, and how they are to be effectively
evangelized is dealt with in chapter six. To read it is an
illuminating experience. The difficulties are clearly set
forth. The various solutions which pastors and mission
executives have thought would work are examined and
evaluated. Then proposals are laid out which will result in
an adequate discipling of the peoples of the transitional
communities.

   Chaney's thesis will encounter opposition, since for
at least fifty years a popular recipe for church advance in
the United States has been to merge several small, weak
churches and make one big beautiful church. Since,
however, he honestly discusses the church merger
formula for advance and points out why it has not worked
and cannot work, his ideas ought to command respect
among churchmen all across the nation, and help
American Christians recognize the bankruptcy of
former ways of dealing with the problem.

   This book will spark a great deal of church planting. It

will rescue the Church from the comfortable belief that only Home Mission Boards can plant new churches. It will create conviction that not only pastors, but laymen and congregations ought constantly to be discipling the peoples and multiplying congregations. American Christianity stands on the edge of a substantial increase of new cells of the body of Christ. This book will play a significant part in bringing about that redemptive forward movement. At the same time, since churches are the most potent instrument of social advance, and the chief factory in which beneficial new social structures are forged, the multiplication of a couple of hundred thousand new congregations will have vast social significance.

Here is a book to read, ponder, give to a friend, study in a class of dedicated Christian men and women, and put *into practice.*

Donald McGavran
Fuller Theological Seminary
Pasadena, California
November 1, 1980

Preface

During the summer of 1954 a few laymen from First Baptist Church in Morganfield, Kentucky, conducted a tent meeting on the edge of their city, out toward the old CCC camp. A number of adults were converted to Christ. Soon a "mission" was opened on the north side of that small county seat because those newly won to faith in Christ didn't feel comfortable at the "big" church, their name for First Baptist. Bankers and county officials, people one had to call "mister," attended there. It made worship and opinion-sharing a threatening experience.

The mother church asked Jim and Carolyn Toler, Marlin Wood, Madlyn Jones, Sally Banks, Louise Jones, Nora Parish, and Bob and Norma Rich, lay leaders in that fellowship, to invest their lives in the new church. I was a first-year student at Southern Baptist Theological Seminary in Louisville and a veteran of three years as pastor of a small church in central Texas. First Baptist Church asked me to become pastor of the new congregation. Later Ed and Frances Walker and Joe and Lucille Farris came to join us from the "big" church. My wife and I moved on "the field" soon and remained there five years. The Northside Baptist Church of Morganfield was born and our entire ministry was shaped by those dedicated lay leaders, that growing new church, and

what God did among us during those years. That episode
in our lives began my long romance with church
planting.

Twelve years followed, first in a "mission" near Ft.
Campbell, Kentucky, and then nine years in a new church
in Palatine, Illinois, a suburb on Chicago's northwest
side. In vastly different contexts we spent seventeen years
in planting and developing new churches.

During our years in suburban Chicago I became
involved with the Chicago Metro Baptist Association
which, with the commitment of young churches like the
one I served, was planting ten or more new congrega-
gations each year during the sixties. Preston Denton was
the inspired leader of that little association of churches. He
is among the most gifted church planters that American
evangelical churches have produced in this century. The
First Baptist Church of Palatine became and is one of the
strongest Southern Baptist churches in the Great Lakes
area, but my most significant achievements while there
were in the new congregations we helped to start.

For the last nine years I have directed a division of
work for the Illinois Baptist State Association. The Church
Extension Division exists principally to assist in the
establishment of new churches. The chapters that follow
have grown out of my study and work during these
years.

Let me express appreciation to Dean Arthur F. Glasser
and Dean Emeritus Donald A. McGavran of the School of
World Missions, Fuller Theological Seminary, for the
invitation to give the annual lectures on church growth at
the School of World Missions in 1979. That opportunity
made it possible for me to get most of this material
together in a manageable form. The faculty, staff, and
student body at Fuller were gracious hosts during the time
these lectures were delivered.

I have spoken on these subjects many times to different
groups. Chapter four was first given at the invitation of
F. Jack Redford at a church extension seminar in Louisville,
Kentucky. Some of the material in chapter two was first
shared with home mission executives and directors of

evangelism serving ecclesiastical bodies in the National Association of Evangelicals. Material in both these chapters as first published in the fall 1978 issue of *Search*.

The work of Eugene Gibson, Abraham Picou, Joseph Rainey, Frank Radcliff, Donald Sharp, and Claude Tears is featured in chapters three and five. I appreciate the cooperation and patience that each of these men has exhibited during the writing process.

In the chapters that follow I have used the word "Church" to refer to the church as the Body of Christ and "church" to refer to a local congregation. I have never used "Church" to refer to a larger ecclesiastical body except in a title like "the United Methodist Church."

James and Dorothy Godsoe have carefully read the manuscript and made valuable suggestions. Dorothy Godsoe has made a substantial contribution by her efforts to make it both readable and accurate. She helped me make these pages say what I intended. Jere Allen and George Bullard, Jr., made several suggestions that have greatly improved chapter six. Harold E. Cameron has read portions of the manuscript and offered helpful suggestions. Helen Williams and Janice Swearingen typed and retyped these pages without a murmur. My wife and daughter have survived another of Dad's big projects with patience and encouragement. For that I am especially thankful.

Thanksgiving Day
November 27, 1980

Acknowledgments

Grateful acknowledgment is given to the following publishers for permission to quote copyrighted material from the titles listed below:

Broadman Press, Nashville, Tennessee, for permission to quote from Talmadge R. Amberson, *The Birth of Churches*, 1979; William O. Carver, *The Glory of God in the Christian Calling*, 1949; Duke K. McCall, editor, *What Is the Church?* 1958; Wayne McDill, *Making Friends for Christ*, 1979; and, F. Jack Redford, *Planting New Churches*, 1979.

Abingdon Press, Nashville, Tennessee, for permission to quote from Robert L. Wilson and James H. Davis, *The Church and the Racially Changing Community*, 1966.

CBS, Inc., New York, New York, for permission to quote K. Livgren, "Dust in the Wind."

Christianity Today, Inc., Wheaton, Illinois, for permission to quote from the June 27, 1980 issue of *Christianity Today*.

Harper and Row, Publishers, New York, for permission to quote from Ezra Earl Jones, *Strategies for New Churches*, 1976.

Home Mission Board, Southern Baptist Convention, for permission to quote from B. Carlisle Driggers, *The Church in the Changing Community: Crisis or Opportunity*, 1977; and Jere Allen and George W. Bullard, Jr., *Hope for the Church in the Changing Community*, 1980.

Moody Press, Chicago, Illinois, for permission to quote from Melvin Hodges, *Build My Church*, 1957.

Princeton Religion Research Center for permission to quote from the June 1979 issue of *Emerging Trends*.

United Methodist Publishing House, Nashville, Tennessee, for permission to quote from the May 1979 issue of *The Circuit Rider.*

William B. Eerdman's Publishers, Grand Rapids, Michigan, for permission to quote from Donald A. McGavran, *Understanding Church Growth,* 1970.

World Wide Publications, Minneapolis, Minnesota, for permission to quote from J. D. Douglas, editor, *Let the World Hear His Voice,* 1975.

Macmillan Publishing Company, Inc., New York, for permission to quote from Michael Novak, *The Rise of the Unmeltable Ethnics,* paperback edition, 1973.

Zondervan Publishing House, Grand Rapids, Michigan, for permission to quote from Harold Lindsell, *An Evangelical Theology of Missions,* 1970.

Noncopyrighted materials in the form of graduate theses, research papers, and lectures have also contributed much to this book. I want to express appreciation for all of these sources and mention some that I have used extensively:

Donald A. McGavran, "Church Growth in America through Planting New Congregations," the closing address of the consultation on evangelism and church growth, October 1976, Kansas City, Missouri; Clay Price and Phillip Jones, "A Study in the Relationship of Church Size and Church Age to Number of Baptisms and Baptismal Rates"; B. Carlisle Driggers, compiler, "Churches in Racially Changing Communities," mimeographed proceedings of the National Leadership Conference, Department of Cooperative Ministries with National Baptists, Home Mission Board, Southern Baptist Convention.

Daniel R. Sanchez, "A Five Year Plan of Growth for the Ministry of the Baptist Convention of New York in the Area of Evangelism," published doctoral dissertation, Fuller Theological Seminary Pasadena, California; George W. Bullard, Jr., "An Analysis of Change in Selected Southern Baptist Churches in Metropolitan Transitional Communities," unpublished Th.M. dissertation, Southern Baptist Theological Seminary, Louisville, Kentucky.

C. Kirk Hadaway, "A Compilation of Southern Baptist Churches and Resident Members Located in Standard Metropolitan Statistical Areas 1978"; and Language Missions Department Home Mission Board, SBC, *America's Ethnicity.*

Scripture quotations are from the *New American Standard Bible,* copyright The Lockman Foundation, 1962, 1963, 1968, 1971, 1972, 1973, 1975.

1

Biblical Pillars
for Church Planting

*The grand object
is to plant
and multiply
self-reliant,
efficient churches,
composed wholly
of native converts,
each church complete
in itself,
with pastor
of the same race
with people.*

Rufus Anderson, 1869

Several years ago, along with two friends,
I spent a week at the Garden Grove Community Church
attending Robert H. Schuller's Institute for Successful
Church Leadership. One morning we spent some time with
Dr. Schuller in his office. It was a memorable few
minutes. One of the things he said went something like
this: "One of the primary reasons that we have been
successful here is that we have learned to ask the right
questions. Asking right questions has priority over
getting right answers. If you do not ask right questions
you cannot get right answers. You may not get right
answers if you ask the right questions, but there is no
possible way—except chance—to get right answers
without them." That made a lot of sense to me.

In 1977, I attended a conference, along with about
100 leaders from various state and national Southern
Baptist Convention (SBC) agencies, concerned
primarily with church growth problems. We addressed
ourselves, for a couple of days, to three questions:

1. *How can we greatly accelerate the beginning of new
   churches all across America?*
2. *How can we penetrate ethnic America with the
   gospel of Christ?*

3. How can we stimulate vitality among churches that have plateaued in growth or are in numerical decline?

I am convinced that those are the right questions. They are questions we must ask today in order to get right answers.

When we asked the question about plateaued and declining churches, we focused on the greatest immediate problem that Southern Baptists and most evangelicals face today. Two questions baffle us. First, why do churches — with Bible in hand and the Holy Spirit indwelling, planted among thousands of responsive people — fail to grow? The second question grows out of the first: How can this pattern be changed?

When we formulated the question about penetrating ethnic America, we identified the major targets for missionary strategy and action in this country. The arena in which we work is a cultural and social complexity. Only recently — and always reluctantly — has this fact been perceived again by denominational leaders. If we do not discover how to penetrate ethnic America, we will miss America.

When we asked the question about greatly multiplying the number of churches, we were addressing a question that is at the heart of the missionary task of the Church of Jesus Christ. We focused on the crucial, specific activity upon which the evangelization of America — in all of its cultural and social complexity — depends. America will not be won to Christ by existing churches, even if they should suddenly become vibrantly and evangelistically alive. Nor will the United States (Canada could also be included) be won to Christ by establishing more churches like the vast majority of those we now have — churches that are predominantly white, or predominantly black, whose members usually speak an easily identifiable American English dialect, and who exhibit (whether white or black) middle-class tastes or magnify middle-class aspirations.

We live in a plural, multi-ethnic, multi-cultural, diverse,

perverse, openly pagan, secular society. Most church leaders are willing to affirm that fact, but few as yet are ready to face its implications for strategy. The United States has always been composed of such a mixture.

There was a period when the dominant culture in America was shaped by one type of Protestantism — the New England variety — and the missionary dream was to impose that cultural pattern on the entire nation and the world. This cultural imperialism was oppressive to many other Protestants, to the most recent immigrants of that period, whether Protestant or Roman Catholic, and to the sectarians.[1]

America is not a Christian nation, but a mission field. The churches here should identify themselves with the young churches of the world and give attention to multiplying congregations among all the social and cultural segments of society.[2] In every population unit — whether census tract, city, county, or state — there are pockets of unchurched people. In some population units, these pockets are huge. In no community are nine-tenths of the population dedicated disciples of Jesus Christ. In most of the communities we have surveyed less than 20 percent of the population meet for worship on a given Sunday. I believe the field is wide open to Southern Baptists, Methodists, Pentecostals, Lutherans, or *any other denomination which will take finding the lost seriously.*

This small book is addressed primarily to the question of accelerating the beginning of new churches. It will become very clear as you read this book that I not only write from the viewpoint of a practitioner but also from the perspective of a Southern Baptist. I write primarily out of my own experience. My research, and especially my illustrations, reflect that experience. However, I have a deep conviction that what I write is germane to *all* Christian denominations. I believe I am writing about the whole American scene. Conversations with other denominational leaders convince me that all ecclesiastical groups in America are experiencing much the same thing. They face almost identical situations. They have many of the same problems and opportunities.

In this first chapter I want to examine with you the biblical foundations upon which I structure my own concern for church planting. This will be a very personal statement from a practitioner. It will explore this question: What are the theological pillars upon which I insist that churches must be multiplied in every segment of society?

THE NATURE AND PURPOSE OF THE CHURCH

The first biblical pillar upon which I base my conviction that churches should be multiplied is the nature and purpose of the Church itself.

THE NATURE OF THE CHURCH. I will not attempt a treatise on the nature of the Church, but I do want to look briefly at three common designations of the Church in the New Testament and what they say about the purpose of the Church, as these designations provide a foundation for aggressive church planting.

The ekklesia *is the* laos *or people of God.* I come from a tradition that has had a very strong emphasis on the local church. In fact Southern Baptists as a whole have been so shaped by the Landmark Movement, which began about 1860, that you cannot really understand us without some comprehension of Landmark principles.[3] Many SBC leaders and influential teachers have insisted that the word *ekklesia* in the New Testament always refers to a local church. A classic statement of this position was written by B. H. Carrol, the founder of South-western Baptist Theological Seminary.[4]

The common Greek word *ekklesia* referred to a local assembly convened for some specific purpose. However, the use of the word by early Christians was informed and conditioned by its use in the Septuagint. There, *ekklesia* was used to refer to the congregation of Israel. It therefore had reference to the people of God. Peter spoke about the Church when he wrote:

*You are a chosen race, a royal priesthood, a holy
nation, a people for God's own possession, that you may
proclaim the excellencies of Him who has called you
out of darkness into His marvelous light; for you once
were not a people, but now you are the people of God;
you had not received mercy, but now you have received
mercy* (1 Pet. 2:9, 10).

Paul, too, spoke of the Church in Titus 2:11-14:

*For the grace of God has appeared, bringing salvation
to all men, instructing us to deny ungodliness and
worldy desires and to live sensibly, righteously and
godly in the present age, looking for the blessed hope and
the appearing of the glory of our great God and Savior,
Christ Jesus; who gave Himself for us, that He might
redeem us from every lawless deed and purify for
Himself a people for His own possession, zealous for
good deeds.*

The people that Christ has purified for his own
possession are the *ekklesia* of God, and the Church is
gathered from "all men." In Acts 15:14, James referred
to the conversion of Cornelius as the way "God first
concerned Himself about taking from among the
Gentiles a people for His name." It is the Father's concern
that a people be gathered for himself from all the
multiplied clans and families of man. If the Church, the
people of God, is to be composed of persons from all
the ethnic groupings of mankind, then local congregations
must be planted among all of these peoples.

The ekklesia *is also the* soma *or Body of Christ.* The
Church is the present physical manifestation of Jesus
Christ the Lord in the world. William O. Carver, the great
Southern Baptist missiologist and New Testament
scholar of the last generation, was bolder than most. He
insisted that the Church is the continuing incarnation
of Christ in the world. "The Church," he said, "is the
extension of his [Christ's] incarnation. A local church is
the manifestation of Christ in its community."[5] In

Ephesians, Carver found the Church "so intimately and
so essentially related to the Christ and to his meaning in
history as to constitute his growing self-realization in
the process of accomplishing the ends of his incarnation.
The Church is his growing Body, that in it he is himself
growing into maturity."[6]

Roland Allen was on target when he said that what we
ultimately seek in our efforts to bring the nations to faith
in Christ is not converts, the multiplication of
congregations, or the Christianization of the social order,
but a manifestation of the character and glory of Christ.[7]
We seek, when we address the gospel to any people, to
manifest the universality, the love and mercy, the glory
and power of Christ. This goal is possible because he is the
hand that fills out the glove of every culture of mankind.
He is the only one who can bring any culture to a true
golden age. And though Allen would say that the
ultimate goal of the mission of the Church is not identical
with the growth of churches, he would also insist that
the manifestation of Christ is achieved through and in the
multiplication of congregations. When we plant
churches among any people, we make it possible for the
character and beauty of Jesus to become incarnate in
that culture. That is how the Church "which is His body,
[becomes] the fulness of Him who fills all in all"
(Eph. 1:23).

Through the process of church planting, the Body of
Christ is brought to its fullness. Ephesians 2:11-22,
rather than being a bulwark against efforts to plant
congregations among all the cultural groupings of
mankind, supports church planting in all the tribes and
families of men. This seminal paragraph describes the
purpose of God in redemption from the point of view of
corporate experience. It speaks of peoples, not individuals.
Through his cross, Jesus has broken down the wall that
divided Jewish peoples from Gentile peoples. The
imagery found in this passage is surely the temple in
Jerusalem. The walls that separated the Gentiles from the
holy place have been destroyed. All the ethnic groupings
of the world now have equal access to the Father.

*So then you are no longer strangers and aliens, but you
are fellow-citizens with the saints, and are of God's
household, having been built upon the foundation of
the apostles and prophets, Christ Jesus Himself being
the corner stone, in whom you also* [as an ethnic group in
Christ, not as an individual] *are being built together into a
dwelling of God in the Spirit* (Eph. 2:19-22).

I especially like W. O. Carver's paraphrase of these verses.

*. . . you are to think of yourselves, in each race group, as
a* structure built upon the *eternal* foundation *of God's
purposes . . .* Christ Jesus Himself being the chief
cornerstone *in the entire structure which God is
building in human history. This structure of a redeemed
humanity is a vast, complex but unitary structure* in
which every distinct building, *as one race group after
another is redeemed,* being harmoniously worked in
with the rest *into the comprehensive architectural plan
of the Great Builder,* makes a growing addition toward a
temple sanctified *in the Lord unto God's glory, thus a
temple* into which you, in your part, are in the process
of being constructed. *The great objective is* to provide a
place of habitation for God, *who* in *his* Spirit *dwells in
this new humanity.*[9]

If it is true that Jesus Christ did purchase for God, with
his blood, men from every tribe and tongue and people
and nation, and has made them to be a kingdom and priests
to our God, and if they are to reign on the earth (Rev.
5:9, 10), then we should get busy gathering into churches
those who say "yes" to the gospel proclamation.

Finally, *the* ekklesia *is the* koinonia *or fellowship of the
Spirit.* In fact, the point could be made that the Holy
Spirit himself does not just create *koinonia* — the
commonality that is ours in Christ — but that he is
himself that *koinonia.* Indeed, it is the Holy Spirit who
makes the Church the living Body of Christ. It is the gift
of the Spirit himself which implants new life in the
believer. He is both the sent and the sending Spirit. He

stirs in the hearts of saints a great desire to share with others what they have discovered in Christ. It is he who enables us to see in others the need which only he can supply. He enables us effectively to pass on to others what we have received. It is he who pushes the Church further and further into the ethnic world. When churches are planted among every segment of society, it is he who unifies us in Christ Jesus. In the Spirit we are all submerged into one body and all made to drink of that same Spirit (1 Cor. 12:13). It is the Holy Spirit, not a super-culture; it is the Holy Spirit, not a sacred, common language; it is the Holy Spirit, not a common organizational structure that makes the Church one. And when churches are planted in the diverse and sometimes antagonistic cultures of mankind, it is the Holy Spirit who makes those human societies into something else — into real manifestations of the Lord Jesus Christ in the world. It was the Holy Spirit who said, "Set apart for Me Barnabas and Saul for the work to which I have called them" (Acts 13:2). Consequently, these men gave themselves to church planting.

If it is the Holy Spirit who gives new life to believers, and if it is the Holy Spirit who makes a church a growing, living organism, and if it is he who is the common ingredient among all Christians, then church planting is at the heart of the mission of the Church. For when churches are planted, the essential nature of the Church, the *koinonia* of the Holy Spirit, is actualized in the world.

THE PURPOSE OF THE CHURCH. Melvin Hodges has said that the Church has a threefold purpose: to evangelize, to edify, and to be God's treasure in the world.[10] If one accepts that simple statement — and I do — it is easy to perceive a threefold ministry for the Church: (1) a ministry to the world of men — to evangelize; (2) a ministry to the body of Christ — to build up; and (3) a ministry to God — to exalt him, to praise and adore him, to be his heritage among the sons of men.

In church planting, we are primarily concerned with

the ministry directed toward the world. How shall we fulfill that purpose? Let me remind you if that purpose is not fulfilled, the Church cannot adequately fulfill the other two purposes.

The big question is: How shall the good news of Jesus Christ be carried effectively to all nations, tribes, clans, and families of men? Certainly, gifted, anointed men will have to cross barriers as pioneers to communicate the message to each of these peoples. But the ultimate method is to plant churches in each of those clans, tribes, and families. Only by seeing that the Church becomes indigenous to every segment of society, to every culture and language of man, can we be reasonably sure that the gospel will effectively touch all the clans of man.

THE NATURE AND CONDITION OF CONTEMPORARY MAN

A second pillar upon which I base my conviction that churches should be multiplied is the nature and condition of contemporary man.

MAN AS FALLEN. Man is not as God made him! I'm grateful and glad that the Bible bears witness to this principle. That truth gives Christians an authentic answer to the pervasive despair that has overcome modern man. Man in his present state is not as God created him. This world is not as God made it. Man is fallen. We are part of a cosmic rebellion. Our sin has shoved the entire universe into tilt. Our world, this created cosmos, is in the bondage of decay. This is the consistent witness of Holy Scripture.

There are far-reaching missionary and evangelistic implications in Francis Schaeffer's often repeated assertion that the prevailing world-view locks contemporary man into unrelieved futility and meaninglessness. According to this assertion, modern man—at least Western man—perceives a universe of natural cause and effect, but a universe that is closed. There can be no intervention from without or within.

The universe is a machine, and man is a robot, inexorably chained to his destiny without any possibility of deliverance.[11]

This perception is demonstrated in many ways. A couple of years ago, the musical group "Kansas" had a song on the charts that is still heard with some regularity. It describes modern despair explicitly.

I close my eyes/Only for a moment and the moment's gone.
All my dreams pass before my eyes — a curiosity.
Dust in the wind,/All we are is dust in the wind.
Same old song,/Just a drop of water in the endless sea./
All we do crumbles to the ground, Though we refuse to see./
Dust in the wind./ All we are is dust in the wind./
Don't hang on./Nothing lasts forever but the earth and sky./
It slips away, and all your money won't another minute buy./
Dust in the wind./ All we are is dust in the wind./
Dust in the wind./ Everything is dust in the wind.[12]

That is not the biblical view of fallen man. The biblical view of man says man indeed is fallen; he is guilty. He is not as God created him, but he can be saved from his despair and restored to the purpose for which he was made.

That is what makes the news about Jesus Christ *good* news. Fallen man not only can be rescued, but he can also be restored to his original purpose.

God had a purpose in creation. This universe and man were not created — as *Green Pastures* suggested — just because the Eternal Father was bored. God always intended to have a big family. His plan was to bring many sons to glory (Heb. 2:10). Jesus Christ is to be the first-born among many brethren (Rom. 8:29). Man was made in the beginning to be in God's family and, being made in his image, to share his life. But man was not just made to be in God's family, he was also created to express God's character, to be *like* God. God wanted not only many children, but also mature sons and daughters. And this is not all! Man was made to have dominion over the earth and its creatures (Gen. 1:26, 27) and, eventually, to reign with Christ over God's entire creation (Rev. 5:10). This was God's original purpose for man. The good news about Jesus Christ, as I said earlier, is that man not only can be rescued from that fallen state, but also can be restored to the ultimate purpose for which he was made.

Let me illustrate this truth. Imagine that you received a letter a few weeks ago from Australia saying that a very wealthy eccentric — of whom you knew nothing — had died and made you his sole heir. His estate was waiting for you to come and claim it. He had left 600,000 acres of Australia's best ranchland, a forty-room modern mansion, a seagoing yacht, and a hundred million dollars after taxes, just to keep it all running. Suppose that you invite me to go along with you to claim your heritage. The two of us are on board an ocean liner crossing the Pacific. It is 300 miles to the nearest island. Suddenly, there is a swell in the sea. The ocean liner is pitched like a leaf in a rain-swept gutter. You lose your footing and are washed overboard.

Our conversation might go something like this:

"Are you all right?" I would yell down to you.

"Help!" would be your reply.

"Can you swim?"

"Help! Help!"

"Listen," I would shout in my most helpful and authoritative voice, "the closest island is 300 miles due north. You had better swim that way. By the way, I would advise you to use the breaststroke."

That may be good advice, but it is bad news! Good news is, "Hang on! Someone is coming to get you." The result would be that you would not only be rescued from the sea, but you would also be returned to the ship and put back on the road to your destiny.

That is the kind of good news that the gospel is: You can be not only rescued but also restored to that high purpose for which God made you in the beginning. That is the gospel and part of the foundation upon which we make disciples and multiply churches.

MAN AS SOCIAL BEING. That man is fallen is not all we need
to say, of course. What I have said is just an effort to portray
something of the hope for fallen man from the biblical
viewpoint. We must also speak of the cultural condition
of humanity. Man's sin alienated him from God, from
himself, from his neighbor, and even from nature. But he
remains a social being. He exists in social structures. He
speaks and hears, he thinks and dreams, within and by
means of particular cultural forms.

It is impossible to communicate with him except
through his own cultural channels. To deny that is to
deny the reality of the human condition. The great
formative missionary task, as I have already indicated, is
to penetrate these social and cultural communities with
the Good News. Our goal is not to tear down and
destroy the structure of culture, but to seek an
incarnation of Christ in each and every particular
culture, to see the character and beauty of Jesus
manifested in each distinct cultural world. That goal is
only achieved when the Church, which is Christ's body, is
growing into his fullness among each people.

Let me make an observation about the growth of
churches and denominations as it is related to cultural,
socio-economic, and racial patterns. I will speak of my
own larger ecclesiastical fellowship — the Southern
Baptist Convention. The particular genius for growth that
Southern Baptists have exhibited in the American South
since about 1880 has been grounded in their ability to
penetrate the various social groupings that were found
there — except, of course, the large black community —
and to plant churches in those various social groupings.
We probably penetrated these groups without a
conscious effort to do so, but we did accomplish it.

Currently, many Convention leaders recognize this
truth. But something else is happening. The South is
becoming increasingly cosmopolitan and pluralistic. Also,
during the last thirty years, Southern Baptists have
exploded outside the boundaries of the Old South into the
complexities of northern and western social patterns.
All of our agencies must develop deliberate, detailed

strategies to penetrate each and every social and cultural community — black, white, and ethnic. My observation is that in spite of our inadequacies at this point, we are probably further along than most large church fellowships in this country. We are making progress. No denominational group in America can be faithful to God without commitment to and integrity in reaching all the peoples that make up America.

Let me respond briefly to two criticisms of this kind of missionary philosophy that I often hear. The first usually comes from those who take pride in traditionalism, holding great respect and appreciation for the past, especially the immediate past. The second comes from those who pride themselves in openness, modernity, and justice. Both, I believe, beg the point.

The first criticism has to do with the way the gospel is packaged. To aim the message at particular groups on the basis of culture is, say the critics, to dilute the message and/or to manipulate the hearers. I am very concerned that the basic message about Jesus Christ not be watered down. I hold that the fundamental biblical tenets are given and authoritative. But we must not confuse the basic message with the cultural wrappings. There are still a few SBC churches in northern Illinois whose message is wrapped and delivered just as it was thirty years ago in northern Alabama, but if these churches were offering their message in Alabama today, no one would be buying.

Adapting the message to the cultural condition of the hearer is not unbiblical. New Testament — specifically Pauline — missionary and evangelistic strategy was avowedly customer-centered.

For though I am free from all men, I have made myself a slave to all, that I might win the more. And to the Jews I became as a Jew, that I might win Jews; to those who are under the Law, as under the Law, though not being myself under the Law, that I might win those who are under the Law; to those who are without law, as without law, though not being without the law of God but under the law of Christ, that I might win those who are without law. To the weak I became weak, that I might win the weak; I have become all things to all men that I may by all means save some (1 Cor. 9:19-22).

Nor is all this crass "manipulation," which is one of today's code words used to castigate aggressive efforts to persuade men to believe in Jesus Christ. Paul wrote in another place to the same people:

We have renounced the things hidden because of shame, not walking in craftiness or adulterating the word of God, but by the manifestation of truth commending ourselves to every man's conscience in the sight of God (2 Cor. 4:2).

Our concern must be with preserving biblical truth not cultural tinsel. But we must be sure that the biblical truth is communicated so that it addresses people as they are and where they are.

The second criticism, of course, is with the homogeneous unit principle. Many responsible Christian leaders see those three words and then read them as R-A-C-I-S-M. The question we often hear is, "Should not Christians be willing to love and receive into their fellowship all kinds of people?" The answer is, of course, "Yes!" Every church should aggressively offer Christ and welcome to full church membership every person within its geographical area who believes in him. But when we come to the matter of church growth — effective evangelism and the multiplication of churches — that is not the question. It is wrong to impose the sophistication or the culture of a mature Christian on a man before he becomes a Christian. He should not be forced to mix in intimate fellowship with those with whom he is uncomfortable in order for him to become a disciple of Jesus.

When we address the question of missionary and evangelistic obedience to Christ, the right question is, "How will the non-Christians most readily receive Christ?" My answer is, "Plant congregations in every

segment of society, so that men and women can find
Christ among their peers without having to give up or
renounce cultural distinctives which have structured a
meaningful life for them in the world. Let the mature
Christian cross the barriers to the unbeliever, not force
the unbeliever to cross the barriers to come to Christ."

The social mosaic that describes the cultural
condition of fallen man becomes, in the Bible, the vehicle
through which God works man's redemption. I was
instructed and encouraged when I discovered in Psalm 86
that it is God who has made the various ethnic groupings
of mankind. Cultural diversity is not a punishment for sin
to be overcome by the cross. God himself made the
nations and has decreed that all are to come and worship
him (Psa. 86:9). The socio-economic and cultural
divisions of mankind are the occasion for the
multiplication of churches and the building of the dwelling
place of God in the Spirit.

THE NATURE AND CHARACTER
OF THE TRIUNE GOD

A third pillar upon which we base our conviction that
churches should be multiplied is the nature and character
of God himself. Many say that the missionary and
evangelistic task of the Church is grounded in the
command of Christ. I believe that the footing of the
missionary character of the Church is more profound
than the commands of Christ that are preserved for us
in Holy Scripture.

There are six distinct biblical statements of our Lord's
commission to the Church. They are extremely
significant and instructive. But should a group of people
on a deserted island find a copy of the epistles of the New
Testament, consequently be converted to Christ, and
have no written account of the commands of Christ, these
people would still have an inner awareness that other
men needed to know Christ. They would sense with
intuitive conviction that they who had been found of
him were under a divine mandate to find others. This is

true because to know Christ is to know the Father and
to have received the Spirit. The missionary task of the
Church has its origin in the nature of the Triune God.[13]

THE PURPOSE OF THE FATHER. Church planting is an
essential, integral part of the mission of the Church, and
the entire missionary task rises out of the ultimate
intention of the Father. W. O. Carver expressed it
romantically seventy years ago, "The origin of missions
is *ultimately* to be found in the heart of God."[14] The
Church and the planting of churches are no trivial
afterthought. They were in God's purpose, to use a phrase
of Spurgeon's, when this world was in the mind of God,
like an oak tree is in the cup of an acorn. It is his purpose
that the whole creation experience redemption and
reconciliation in Christ (Col. 1:20) and "be set free from
its slavery to corruption into the freedom of the glory
of the children of God" (Rom. 8:21). That hope waits on
the "revealing of the sons of God" (Rom. 8:19).
According to God's purpose, Abraham was called, and the
nation of Israel was chosen. It was the intention of the
Father that his own Son should become flesh and be
delivered up to death "by the predetermined plan and
foreknowledge of God" (Acts 2:23). It was God's purpose
to raise him from the dead. It is also God's purpose that
the Church of Jesus Christ take this message of redemption
and reconciliation to every people and tribe on the face
of the globe.

THE LORDSHIP OF CHRIST. Church planting is also grounded in
the lordship of Jesus Christ. God has made him both
Lord and Christ (Acts 2:36). He is seated at the right hand
of God in heavenly places. He is far above all other
rulers and authorities and powers. He is made head over all
things to the Church (Eph. 1:20-23). All authority and
power has been given to him (Matt. 28:18). "God highly
exalted Him, and bestowed on Him the name which is
above every name, that at the name of Jesus every knee
should bow, of those who are in heaven, and on earth,
and under the earth, and that every tongue should

confess that Jesus Christ is Lord, to the glory of God the Father" (Phil. 2:9-11).

Jesus Christ is Lord! The nations have been given to him for a heritage (Psa. 2:8). Our task is to claim for him what is his. The decisive battle has been fought. The invader and usurper have been defeated. The final outcome is sure. Christ must reign until all things are put under his feet (1 Cor. 15:25). The Kingdom of God came to this age in the life, death, and resurrection of Christ. Jesus erected and then empowered his Church. The Church is the instrument of the Kingdom of God, which works through the Church. It is the community of the Kingdom of God. It presses the battle against satanic evil in the world and controls the keys that open the door to eternal life. Local congregations are intended to be outposts of the Kingdom, where the doors to the Kingdom are swung wide and where spiritual warfare is carried on.[15] Church planting is an expression of the concern that the way into the Kingdom be opened for all men, for every tribe and subtribe of humanity. It is part of the process of actualizing the lordship of Christ in the world.

THE MINISTRY OF THE SPIRIT. Finally, church planting is grounded in the ministry of the Holy Spirit. "Methods alone, even correct methods, will not produce a New Testament church. The mechanics of proper procedure must be accompanied by the dynamics of apostolic power."[16] "New churches are born . . . because the Holy Spirit of God is still at work in . . . [the] world. Indeed, apart from the work of the Holy Spirit there would be no new churches."[17] The Bible punctuates the truth of these statements. Church planting is precisely the work of the Spirit. For, as I have said earlier, it is he who creates community; he is the commonality of the Church and the churches. It is in and through churches that the Spirit performs his ministry. The history of missions in its totality is the history of the work of the Spirit of God.[18]

Church planting is grounded in the ministry of the Spirit in at least four ways. First, *the Holy Spirit indwells the gathered congregation as well as the body of the*

believer. His indwelling presence makes a church a
living organism. He is, therefore, absolutely essential to the
birth of a church. A crowd of people, meeting in one
place, even to worship the true and living God, is not by
the act of gathering constituted as a church. Even if the
Word is preached and the sacraments observed, these
alone do not transform a group of believers into a body
in Christ. That is uniquely the work of the Holy Spirit.

Secondly, *the Holy Spirit instructs churches.* This is
just what happened at Antioch in Acts 13. The Holy
Spirit gave clear directions. "Set apart for Me Barnabas
and Saul for the work to which I have called them"
(Acts 13:2). It is the Holy Spirit that moves upon a
congregation and calls individuals from that congregation
to a ministry of church planting.

This last phrase leads into the third way that church
planting is grounded in the ministry of the Spirit. *The
Holy Spirit endows churches.* Through the gifts given by
the Holy Spirit a church is enabled to function properly
and effectively. It is time we gave up our identification of
the Twelve as the only apostles and recognize the
apostolic gift as still present in the Church. When a church
becomes committed to church planting, God invariably
raises up believers who are endowed with this gift and
who prove very productive in church planting.

Finally, *the Holy Spirit empowers churches.* He mediates
the power of the Lord Christ to his people. Anyone who
has been involved in trying to gather a church out of the
pagan pools of American society can testify to the
absolute necessity of the direct intervention of the Holy
Spirit in this work. The Spirit was poured out after Christ
was exalted to the right hand of God. He is the dynamic
force of vital Christian life. New churches will never be
planted until those charged with gathering them learn to
appropriate the power available through the Holy Spirit.
"The Spirit of God," John R. Mott wrote seventy years
ago, "is the great missioner [he could have said "church
planter"] and . . . only as He dominates the work and
workers can we hope for success."[19] Church planting is
grounded in the ministry of the Spirit because the

essential ministries of the Holy Spirit are essential to the church planting process.

How shall I conclude this? I believe it is important to ask the right questions. I also believe it is important to operate from a strong biblical base. I have a deep conviction that God wants us to multiply churches in every segment of society in these last years of the twentieth century — both in America and around the world.

NOTES

[1]For a more detailed discussion, see Charles Chaney, "Garden or Wilderness: The Mission to America in Historical and Personal Perspective," *The Birth of Missions in America* (South Pasadena, CA: William Carey Library, 1976), pp. 281-304.

[2]See Franklin H. Littell, *From State Church to Pluralism* (Garden City, NY: Anchor Books; Doubleday and Company, Inc., 1962), pp. 29-36.

[3]See *Baptist History and Heritage,* Vol. X (January, 1975), No. 1, an excellent introduction to Landmarkism and its relationship to the Southern Baptist Convention.

[4]B. H. Carrol, *Baptists and Their Doctrines* (New York: Fleming H. Revell Company, 1913), pp. 37-62.

[5]W. O. Carver, "Introduction," in Duke K. McCall, *What Is the Church?* (Nashville: Broadman Press, 1958), p. 3.

[6]W. O. Carver, *The Glory of God in the Christian Calling* (Nashville: Broadman Press, 1949), p. 43.

[7]Roland Allen, *Missionary Principles* (Grand Rapids: Wm. B. Eerdmans Publishing Company, 1964), pp. 67-100.

[8]*Ibid.,* p. 93.

[9]*Glory of God,* p. 201.

[10]Melvin Hodges, *A Guide to Church Planting* (Chicago: Moody Press, 1973), p. 16.

[11]See Francis Schaeffer, *The Church at the End of the 20th Century* (Downers Grove, IL: Inter Varsity Press, 1970), pp. 9-25, for example.

[12]K. Livgren, "Dust in the Wind," on Kansas, *The Kirsher,* LP album, CBS Record, CBS, Inc., 51 W. 52 Street, New York, NY).

[13]See Leslie Newbigin, *Trinitarian Faith and Today's Mission* (Richmond, VA: John Knox Press, 1964).

[14]W. O. Carver, *Missions in the Plan of the Ages* (New York: Fleming H. Revell Company, 1909), p. 12.

[15]George Eldon Ladd, *The Gospel of the Kingdom* (Grand Rapids: Wm. B. Eerdmans Publishing Company, 1918), p. 117.

[16]Melvin Hodges, *Build My Church* (Chicago: Moody Press, 1957), p. 97.

[17]J. Terry Young, "The Holy Spirit and the Birth of Churches," in *The Birth of Churches,* Talmadge R. Amberson, ed., (Nashville: Broadman Press, 1979), p. 163.

[18]Harold Lindsell, *An Evangelical Theology of Missions* (Grand Rapids: Zondervan Publishing House, 1970), p. 190.

[19]John R. Mott, *The Decisive Hour of Christian Missions* (New York: Laymen's Missionary Movement, 1910), p. 193.

2

Developing a Regional Strategy in Church Planting

The multiplication of
soundly Christian churches
throughout all segments
of society,
throughout
all homogeneous units,
till every people,
every ethnic unit is
seeded with churches,
is . . . a procedure
well pleasing to God.

Donald A. McGavran, 1980

For most of this century, and especially during the last two decades, Christian leaders have deprecated the need for new churches in America. In an age that has emphasized social action and ecumenical interests, the romance has been with church mergers, not church planting, and with the application of the gospel to the various issues and systems of society, not the gathering of churches in the various segments of society.

This pattern has characterized most evangelicals as well as conciliar Protestants.

"Church extension" became a loaded phrase, more closely related in the minds of many to denominational empire-building than to the mission of the Church of Jesus Christ. "Church planting," a more biblical and acceptable term, has now come into use. "Church planting" is used in these chapters to refer to those things one existing Christian fellowship does to share its faith in Jesus Christ with another community of people and to form them into a new congregation of responsible disciples of Jesus Christ.[1] The fellowship of Christians may be members of a local church or agents of a missionary board, society, or association. Church planting is preeminently an apostolic task, and it is central to the mission of the Church.

Space and time do not allow documentation of the need for new churches in America.[2] There are 80 million people in the United States who do not claim to have an allegiance to any Christian group. There are only six other nations that have a total population larger than 80 million. This makes America one of the great mission fields of the world. It is absurd to think that those 80 million, plus another 90 million who are affiliated with Christian churches but are nonresident and/or inactive, are going to be adequately discipled by existing churches. Most of the 80 million are socially and culturally removed from the homogeneous units in which the majority of existing churches are established. New churches must be planted if these peoples are to be brought to personal faith in Christ and responsible membership in his church.

At least two major problems hinder the various denominational bodies in America from taking the church planting task seriously. First, there is often no national or regional strategy for church planting to which the group is committed. What is done is piecemeal and projected on the basis of communities of people already won to faith in Christ and committed to a certain theological and/or doctrinal position. Seldom is a strategy designed to plant churches in the large unchurched communities that are all around us.

Second, there is no climate within local churches for them to become actively involved in extension and bridging growth.[3] Local churches resist the idea of planting daughter churches in another city (or town) or another section of their city among people in essentially the same homogeneous groups as their own. Further, many local churches do not get excited about planting daughter churches among people who are a significant cultural or racial distance from themselves.

This chapter is addressed to the first of these problems. Confident that our experience in Illinois will be of extreme interest to most other denominational groups, especially to those ecclesiastical leaders

responsible for new church development, this chapter
is a report on what the churches of the Illinois Baptist State
Association (IBSA) did from March 1973 through
December 1976. During that period 100 new church-type
congregations were added to our fellowship. This
chapter will also describe the planning procedure of the
North Central States Mission Thrust, a twelve-year effort
to double the number of Southern Baptist churches in a
seven-state area around the western Great Lakes.

CHURCH PLANTING IN ILLINOIS

THE HERITAGE OF ILLINOIS BAPTISTS. The Illinois Baptist State
Association is a convention of approximately 1,025
congregations in Illinois, with about 225,000 members,
created, according to the 1969 constitution, to "assist in
establishing and developing Baptist churches." When
the IBSA was formed in 1907 by 226 churches that had
withdrawn from the Illinois State Baptist Convention,
its constitution stated that the "leading objects of this
Association shall be the planting and supporting of
Baptist churches in the State of Illinois." Except for one
church in Zion founded in 1917, four or five little
churches around the Calumet Harbor begun in the thirties
and forties, and about fifty churches immediately west
and south of Springfield, almost all of the IBSA churches
were located in the southern one-third of the state. This
situation continued for about forty years. Messengers of
IBSA churches were seated at the Southern Baptist
Convention in 1910.

By the end of World War II, there were 573 churches.
After 1945, churches began to be planted at various places
in central and northern Illinois, and in 1950 an intensive
and deliberate effort was begun to start new churches all
over the state. Between 1945 and 1970, there was a net
increase of 312 churches. Many more than that were
established, but attrition in rural southern Illinois held
the net increase down.

In addition to the Illinois churches, about seventy-five new churches were planted in Indiana, Minnesota, and Wisconsin. Membership during that same twenty-five year period increased from 89,000 to 191,000.

The missionary method during this period was much the same as that used in the formative years of the Baptist General Conference, the Evangelical Free Church of America, and the missionary team sent out from the church in Antioch during the first century. The plan was to find a couple of families from "down home"—people who said "y'all" and ate cornbread—get them in a Bible study, let them invite their friends and extended family members, and then watch the Lord save some and reclaim others. Soon twenty-five to fifty members would become a nucleus for forming a church. Invariably, some of the families reached for Christ would be from a nearby town or a different community in the city. So, the new, baby congregation—enthusiastic and excited—would start a "mission" in that place, in the home of a family from their fellowship. The process would start all over again. In this manner, the Harvey Missionary Baptist Church of Harvey, Illinois, became the mother church to about twenty congregations. The Larkin Avenue Baptist Church in Elgin sponsored ten new churches in the first ten years of its existence.

Who led these churches? Laymen and men who had felt an inward call to preach. These latter had been licensed and/or ordained; they were with or without formal training. But they moved to one of these communities and "made tents." Actually, very few were really tentmakers! However, many were carpenters, school teachers, and factory workers. Even today 50 percent of our pastors in Illinois continue to be bivocational.

By 1965, most of those clusters of similar-culture prospects had already been found and penetrated. The formation of new churches leveled off. IBSA had a net increase of only thirty-five churches between 1965 and 1972. This situation demanded a new missionary strategy.

A NEW MISSIONARY STRATEGY. In March 1973, the Board of Directors of IBSA authorized a three-year program (1974-1976) called *ExtendNow to All of Illinois.* It was designed to mobilize all IBSA churches in a united, voluntary effort to extend their ministry and witness to all parts (places) and all populations (peoples) in the state.

This action grew out of a strong conviction that pervades our fellowship, that Christians are under a divine order not only to offer Jesus Christ to all men, but also to plant evangelistic churches in every nook and corner of this land. During the last quarter century, as I noted in the first chapter, there has been the growing realization that this means not one church in every place, but multiple churches where there are significant racial, socio-economic, and cultural patterns.

The particular objectives and goals of *ExtendNow* were based on information gathered in a study of 1970 Census data related to the number and location of IBSA churches and the number of resident members in those churches.

With the assistance of Dr. Tommy Coy of the Planning Section of the Home Mission Board in Atlanta, a formula was devised by which we could, through the use of a computer, determine a Geographical Extension Index (G.E.I.) for every place in Illinois that would indicate probable need for new churches.

In addition to a realistic estimate of the need for new churches in a community, we also wanted to know something about the demographic, socio-economic, and ethnic character of each community. We therefore wrote a computer program that not only gave the G.E.I., but also provided information on each community in reference to:

1. *Number of IBSA churches*
2. *Number of IBSA resident members*
3. *Total population*
4. *Percent change in population 1960-1970*
5. *Percent non-white population*

6. *Percent ethnic population*
7. *Percent non-English speaking in the home*
8. *Percent single, separated, or divorced*
9. *Percent 65 or over*
10. *Percent owner-occupied housing under $15,000*
11. *Percent owner-occupied housing over $35,000*
12. *Percent of housing rented*
13. *Percent of living in multiple family units*
14. *Percent of families with income above $15,000*
15. *Percent of families under federal poverty level*
16. *Percent in professional occupations*
17. *Percent in labor occupations.*

With this data we had a good preliminary profile on each place. We then gathered all of this information from six perspectives:

1. *total population*
2. *total population of each of the 102 counties in the state*
3. *total rural population of each county*
4. *total urban population of each county*
5. *every city in Illinois with 2,500 or more population*
6. *each of the 76 distinct communities in Chicago.*

This provided an excellent factual base on which to develop a statewide strategy.

The formula for discovering the G.E.I. was as follows:

$$G.E.I. = 1/3 \left[\frac{2(P70)}{C71} + \frac{(P70)}{M71} \right]$$

where: P = population in each place
C = number of churches in each place
M = number of members in each place

The G.E.I. is a score given to each place on the basis of the ratio of IBSA churches in 1971 (C71) to the population in 1970 (P70) and the ratio of IBSA resident members in 1971 (M71) to the population in 1970. Each of these ratios was given an arbitrary value.

**Arbitrary Value for
Population per
Church Ratio**
1, if 1:1999 or less
2, if 1:2000-3999
3, if 1:4000-5999
4, if 1:6000-7999
5, if 1:8000-9999
6, if 1:10000-11999
7, if 1:12000-13999
8, if 1:14000-15999
9, if 1:16000-17999
10, if 1:18000 or more,
   or if no churches
   located in the area

**Arbitrary Value for
Population per
Member Ratio**
1, if 1:19 or less
2, if 1:20-39
3, if 1:40-59
4, if 1:60-79
5, if 1:80-99
6, if 1:100-119
7, if 1:120-139
8, if 1:140-159
9, if 1:160-179
10, if 1:180 or more,
   or if no members are
   located in the area

Because we felt that the presence of a church was of more relative importance than the number of church members, we doubled the value of the church-to-population ratio. Since the uppermost arbitrary value was ten for each ratio, we divided the sum of the two ratios by three, which resulted in a G.E.I. for each place between one and ten.

CHURCH PLANTING NEEDS IN ILLINOIS. The results of this survey were overwhelming. Although we were second only to United Methodists among Protestants in number of churches and members in Illinois, we found that there were many places and many population pockets we were overlooking.

1. Twenty-six counties—all in northern Illinois— had great church extension needs (G.E.I. of 10.0). Twenty additional counties had large enough ratios of IBSA Christians and churches to pull the G.E.I. below 7.0.

2. One hundred and ten small cities (2,500-10,000) had no IBSA church. Sixty-six other small cities had only one church with less than 200 members.

3. Fifty-one medium cities (10,000-50,000) had no IBSA church. Sixty other medium cities had only one IBSA church, which had less than 300 members.

4. Six large cities (50,000-150,000) had no IBSA

church. Seven other large cities had only one or two IBSA churches, which had an average membership of 150.

5. Thirty IBSA churches existed in the city of Chicago in 1971, but those were located in only nineteen of the seventy-six communities. There were fifty-seven significant "cities" inside Chicago in which we had no organized work.

6. The survey revealed a varied ethnic population of 2,000,000, growing rapidly, especially among Spanish-speaking groups. We had barely begun to penetrate those different ethnic populations.

7. We discovered a black community in Illinois of 1,400,000 in which we had no strategy for evangelism or church planting.

8. We discovered 159 towns (1,000-2,500) and 256 villages (500-1,000) in which we had no organized witness.

9. It was obvious that the Chicago Standard Metropolitan Statistical Area (SMSA) demanded our greatest effort and resources. It had 62.8 percent of the population of the state and only 15 percent of our churches. Sixty-one of the small cities, forty-seven of the medium cities, five of the large cities, and all fifty-seven of the Chicago communities where we had no organized witness were in this SMSA. The bulk of the ethnic and black communities were located there.

We adopted a strategy with five overarching objectives and fifteen distinct goals. One of those goals was to add 100 churches or church-type congregations to our fellowship by 1976. We set out to do a more detailed profile of every place in Illinois with a population of more than 500. Only in this way could we discover if there was an adequate evangelistic witness in these various places. This was a long process that we did not totally complete. We did profile hundreds of places. We found an inadequate witness to Christ characteristic of most communities. In some towns as few as 13 percent of the population are in a church on a given Sunday. If all the alleged church members were to go to church on a given Sunday, more than twice the number of available seats would be required. In many places there was competition among various churches. But the competition was for the middle or upper middle-class families. Few efforts were being made to reach the "poor folks" except by Pentecostals, a few Holiness churches, and some Baptists.

As I have already indicated, in forty-four months we counted exactly 100 new churches or church-type congregations. Of that 100, twelve either failed or did not follow through with official affiliation with IBSA and/or one of the thirty-four local associations within our state. At the end of the period, nine might legitimately have been called "Bible fellowships," not having reached the full phase of "mission" or "chapel" status. Our net increase was seventy-nine. Eighteen of those were in the black communities of Illinois, and twenty-eight were in eleven different language culture groups.

CHURCH PLANTING PRINCIPLES. The question is, of course, how did we do this? My answer is: *Any and every way we could!* It was accomplished through a broad involvement of local churches, an extensive use of volunteers, the efforts of a few catalytic missionaries, the ministries of many bivocational preachers, the allocation of limited supportive funds, and the efforts of a very small number of fully salaried church planters. We were doctrinaire about the insignificance of permanent sites and buildings for new churches. We were unashamed of small churches and unafraid of failure. We seriously attempted to maintain broad prayer support for the entire effort. And, all the time we trained, encouraged, evangelized, propagandized, baptized, and prophesied wherever we were. In short, church planting takes dedication, spelled W-O-R-K.

Let me give a word of explanation about some of these factors.

1. Missionary responsibility, in our view, does not rest in the Church Extension Division of IBSA, the Home Mission Board of the Southern Baptist Convention (SBC) nor with any board or society organized for missionary

purposes. It belongs to the local church. We take that
very seriously. We begin no new work without local
church sponsorship of some kind. To start 100 new
churches, we have had far more than 100 sponsoring
churches involved to some degree. Missionary
responsibility is diffused to the grassroots.

2. All but about ten IBSA churches are affiliated with a
local association of churches, such as the Chicago
Metropolitan Baptist Association, Oak Park. There is no
organic or organizational relationship between IBSA
and these local associations. Twenty-three have full-time
directors of missions. Some of these men serve in areas
where new churches are most needed, and they have
been catalytic agents in church planting. IBSA also has
five men located over the state who serve in a catalytic
capacity, in addition to a director of a Language Missions
Department and a director of a Missions Department. My
immediate subordinates and I try to be directly or
indirectly involved in starting a new church each year.

3. Volunteers have been used by the hundreds to
cultivate new church communities. Youth choir groups,
mission groups, individual adults, and college and
seminary students who give a summer or semester have all
played a part. They come mostly at their own expense
and without remuneration. Several youth choirs, after
one or two weeks in a community, have been able to
leave in existence a new Bible fellowship or, on occasion, a
new mission or chapel. Missionary partnerships
between local associations in southern Illinois and those
in northern Illinois have been formed, so that the
resources of each can be shared to meet various mission
goals — primarily through volunteers.

4. Many of the baby churches are nurtured and
developed by lay preachers or by men who have
experienced God's call to preach after they already had
families and careers. Some have had theological training,
and some have not. They work at various vocations and
"bootleg" the gospel. Such a man leads a new church
part-time until it grows beyond him, or until it can assume
his support and that of his family. A few continue to be

bivocational pastors of large churches with multiple
staffs. This method has been most effective in small
towns in Illinois, where the old line denominations have
consolidated or withdrawn, leaving a vacuum for an
evangelistic witness, and in the ethnic and black
communities. We conduct a school for training lay
preachers among the Spanish-speaking and another for
providing college credit in Bible and religious education
courses for lay persons and pastors without theological
training.

It is my own personal conviction that the 1,000 new
churches we will begin in Illinois during the balance of
this century will be led by men like these, rather than
those with more professional ministerial training.
Availability is far more important than capability.

5. Monetary support of new churches and missions
is, when all things are considered, minimal. When we put
men on Church Pastoral Aid (CPA), only rarely did IBSA
contribute as much as $500 per month. Under the
program, a man gives full time to his work, and the new
church and the sponsoring church or chapel must
provide the remainder of the salary. The aid decreases
over five years until full support by the church is achieved.
Most churches achieve this self-support in less than five
years. Language Pastoral Assistance (LPA) has been a little
more lenient, but we are moving rapidly toward the
same general guidelines for both CPA and LPA. Our total
subsidy support over forty-four months was about
$650,000. This included new churches as well as those
already receiving CPA and LPA before *ExtendNow*
began.

The Home Mission Board, SBC, works in Illinois in a
cooperative arrangement through the Church Extension
Division, IBSA. We do cooperative budget and program
planning. The HMB participates at a 60/40 ratio in our
total budget, including staff salaries. In 1976, that total
budget was $443,000. Besides dollar participation, HMB
personnel provide valuable assistance in placing,
training, and recruiting volunteers and staff. The HMB,
however, only participated in about $450,000 of the

forty-four months' subsidy. The remainder was given in Illinois.

6. The total subsidy for forty-four months included a small number of fully salaried church planters. These are men with experience and/or training whom we have located in strategic communities with a livable salary. They usually go into a community to begin from scratch. We ultimately had thirteen such men during the forty-four-month period—three in ethnic communities, two in black communities, and eight in white, English-speaking communities. These men accounted for 15 percent of the new units we began.

7. The availability of a permanent building or building site is never a prerequisite or determinitive to beginning a new church. Get the people, you can get a place. God's people, led by God's man, can produce the facilities that are needed. We are now able to provide some seed money for a down payment on property, but that was not a feature of *ExtendNow.*

8. Numbers of small churches that need to grow do not keep us from beginning other new churches. IBSA has a full division of Church Development. We have the conviction that churches always begin small. If you multiply churches in your fellowship, you must expect to have small churches around.

Nor does the fear of failure deter us. Some new churches do not survive, and some exist only a few years. We hold doggedly to principles of local church autonomy. We have some new churches that decide not to affiliate with us. We regret this, but hold no strings that would compel affiliation.

9. We see the whole effort of church planting as a spiritual ministry done effectively only in the power of the Holy Spirit. We therefore pray much and enlist and train others to pray much. The IBSA staff members preach often, witness, and do soul-winning in all kinds of places, and in other ways invest our lives personally in these budding new congregations. We, with many others, plant and water, but we count on God to give the increase.

CHURCH PLANTING IN SEVEN
NORTH CENTRAL STATES

This method of identifying church planting needs on a more scientific basis was picked up in 1973 by the executive directors and missions directors of the SBC state conventions in Ohio, Michigan, Indiana, and Illinois, in a joint planning effort. Because the SBC churches in these four midwestern states share many similar problems, these men had been meeting each January for several years for fellowship and discussion of common needs. When the results of the survey in Illinois were shared, a decision was made to join together in a significant step forward—especially in church planting—in these Great Lakes states.

The North Central States Mission Thrust (NCSMT) has three purposes: (1) to double the number of churches, missions, and organized ministries in the region by 1990; (2) to focus the attention of SBC on the region for a significant period of time—1977-1990; and (3) to assist in turning the resources of all SBC agencies to meet priority mission needs in the region.

The Iowa and Minnesota-Wisconsin Fellowships of Southern Baptist Churches soon joined with the four state conventions. The base date for counting was made October 1, 1973. At that time, there were 1,738 churches in the seven-state area, and 180 church-type chapels that had not yet become independently organized churches. Sixty-six months later the total had risen to 1,984 churches and 342 church-type chapels. On December 16, 1979, the two-thousandth Southern Baptist church within these seven north central states was organized in Milford, Michigan.

At this point we are disappointed in our achievements, and realize we will have to pick up the pace dramatically if we are to double the number of churches by 1990. Nevertheless, a good question remains: How have we gone about developing a seven-state strategy in church planting?

We have been somewhat successful in enlisting SBC

agencies to concentrate their energy, imagination, technology, and resources in a sustained effort for advance in church planting in this strategic, populous, and generally responsive region.

DEVELOPING A PLANNING BASE. First, we developed a common planning base for the seven states. We went to the Planning Section of the Home Mission Board, and they developed a data-gathering model—much like the one used in Illinois. It was adjusted because of the much larger population and number of places in the seven-state area. The model was designed to delineate communities of people in the north central states (NCS) that were in need of a church, a church-type mission, or a special ministry to certain groups of people.

The model was developed on three assumptions:

1. The model had to be flexible enough to consider the presence of existing SBC units of work, both large and small, and the diversity and distribution of the population.

2. The model had to be built on the same geographical base as the existing church and population data. The most compatible base consisted of places and county boundaries grouped into appropriate population categories. We gathered data as follows:

Counties, Total Population	*623 Counties*
Places of 1,000,000 or more	*2 Places*
Places of 500,000-1,000,000	*4 Places*
Places of 250,000-500,000	*5 Places*
Places of 100,000-250,000	*21 Places*
Places of 50,000-100,000	*61 Places*
Places of 25,000-50,000	*140 Places*
Places of 10,000-25,000	*346 Places*
Places of 5,000-10,000	*409 Places*
Places of 2,500-5,000	*546 Places*
Counties, Rural Population	*623 Counties*

3. Since the major unit work was that of churches, the model had to be built on a base which would show the need for new churches by a single geographical

index score. To help indicate the need for special types of churches and to reflect the need for special ministries, support data was gathered alongside the geographical index score when it reached a certain predetermined point for a specific condition. This support data included racial, cultural, social, economic, and housing data.

The geographical indicators included the number of SBC churches in each place, the number of resident members in these churches, and the total population of each place. The support indicators which helped understand the social character of each place and which helped identify the need for social or cross-cultural ministries were as follows:

1. *Percentage net change in population, 1960-70, if 25 percent or above.*
2. *Percentage of total population, non-white, if 20 percent or above.*
3. *Percentage of total population, ethnic, if 20 percent or above.*
4. *Percentage of total population with mother-tongue other than English, if 20 percent or above.*
5. *Percentage of population fourteen years or over, single, separated, widowed or divorced, if 15 percent or above.*
6. *Percentage of population sixty-five years and over, if 15 percent or above.*
7. *Percentage of occupied housing units renter occupied, if 40 percent or above.*
8. *Percentage of housing units not single-unit structures, if 40 percent or above.*
9. *Percentage of families with income over $15,000, if 30 percent or above.*
10. *Percentage of families under poverty level, if 15 percent or above.*
11. *Percentage of employed persons sixteen years and over in professional and administrative professions, if 30 percent or above.*
12. *Percentage of employed persons sixteen years and over in laborer occupations, if 25 percent or above.*

The data-gathering model was a formula much like the one developed for Illinois. It was limited in that it only pointed to possible trends and above-average possibilities which might call for new units of work. It looked like this:

$$\text{Geographical Extension Index (G.E.I.)} = 1/3 \left[2\left(\frac{P70}{C73}\right)_{av_1} \left(\frac{P70}{M73}\right)_{av_2} \right]$$

where: P = population of each place

      C = number of churches in each place

      M = number of church members in each place

      av = arbitrary value assigned to various ratios

DATA FINDINGS. What conclusions did we draw from this statistical look at the area?

1. *The north central states (NCS) are crucial for a national strategy.* The seven states which compose this region are a vital part of the great agricultural belt across the Great Plains, but 75 percent of the population live in urban areas. These states contain the second largest metropolitan cluster in America; only that along the northeastern seaboard is larger. The population in the NCS in 1970 was 46,881,877, or 23 percent of the population of the nation. Almost one out of four people who live in the USA live in these seven states.

2. *The region has tremendous church planting needs.* Twenty percent of the 47 million population live in eleven cities of over 250,000. Among the almost 10 million people in these cities Southern Baptists had only 124 churches in 1972. That amounts to a ratio of more than 100,000 people for each SBC church. This would be approximately the same ratio as if there were only a total of sixty-two SBC churches in Atlanta, Birmingham, Dallas, Houston, Louisville, Memphis, Miami, New Orleans, and Oklahoma City combined!

There were twenty-one cities with a population between 100,000 and 250,000 — a total population of over three million. There were 109 SBC churches in these cities — a ratio of 1 to 30,000. This would be comparable to a situation where there would be only 109 SBC churches for all of Kentucky!

There were 201 cities in the NCS with a population between 25,000 and 100,000. They had a combined population of over 9 million with 231 SBC churches—a ratio of 1 to 40,000. This would be equivalent to having only 121 SBC churches in Tennessee and Georgia combined, or to having one church for Jackson, Tennessee.

Finally, there were 3,301 small cities in the NCS with populations ranging between 2,500 and 25,000. The total population of these cities was 10,000,000—almost identical to the total of the eleven very large cities. There were 337 SBC churches in these cities—a ratio of one to 18,000.

In the survey we identified every place in the NCS with a population above 2,500, as well as doing a study of the total population and rural population by counties. There were 1,534 cities with a population in excess of 2,500 in these seven states; 1,014 had a G.E.I. of 10.0. There were 623 counties in the seven state area; 418 had a G.E.I. of 10.0. This does not take into account the large number of places with G.E.I. of 7.0 to 9.9. These also had significant church planting needs.

There are, of course, other Baptists and other evangelical Christians in the NCS. There are *many strong, evangelistic churches* in this region. This is also true where Southern Baptists are strongest! In fact, there are more evangelical churches per 1,000 population where Southern Baptists are strongest than in these seven states. We did a comparison between two cities in Illinois of approximately the same size—Marion and Buffalo Grove, Illinois. Marion is in southern Illinois, where Southern Baptists have been strong all of this century. In this city of 10,000 there were five SBC churches, one American Baptist, one Freewill Baptist, one National Baptist, one American Baptist Association, and one General Baptist. There were also two Methodist, one Presbyterian, five Pentecostal, one Catholic, one Episcopal, one Lutheran, one Reformed Latter Day Saints, one Jehovah Witness, etc.—thirty-two churches in all. Buffalo Grove, in suburban Chicago, was atypical in that it had two small Baptist churches—one

affiliated with the North American Baptist General
Conference and one with the General Association of
Regular Baptists. In addition, it had one Catholic, one
United Church of Christ, and one Methodist church, and a
Jewish synagogue. If all the Southern Baptists in Marion
were removed, there would still be more Baptists and
other evangelicals there than in Buffalo Grove. This is
the typical pattern.

As you can imagine, this information has been highly
motivational. It has also provided each state convention
with a data base upon which to do planning during this
decade. It has been helpful in identifying geographical,
socio-economic, and cultural communities that might be
ripe for church planting ministries.

But we discovered another way to look at the region.
Using information gathered from ninety-two different
denominational groups in America, the Planning Section
of the Home Mission Board fed into the computer the
basic information about numbers of churches and
resident members for each county in the United States.
They were then able to develop an Evangelism Index
and Church Index for each county. Using this data, we
were able to compare the situation of Southern Baptists
in the seven north central states with Southern Baptists in
seven south central states (Alabama, Arkansas, Kentucky,
Louisiana, Mississippi, Missouri, and Tennessee). Here is
what we discovered:

	NCS	SCS
Total Population	46,881,877	23,044,572
SBC Churches	1,782	14,115
SBC Members	420,913	5,439,390
Other Baptist Churches	7,569	8,762
Other Baptist Members	2,421,504	2,242,000
Other Evangelical Churches	10,115	6,605
Other Evangelical Members	2,915,403	939,134
Other Protestant Churches	24,599	16,617
Other Protestant Members	9,773,108	3,628,462
Catholic Churches	6,471	2,129
Catholic Members	12,646,463	2,794,191

Sectarian Congregations	762	386
Sectarian Members	180,966	100,576
Non-Christian Congregations	403	157
Non-Christian Members	640,586	138,894
Unaffiliated with any group	17,782,878	7,607,925
Language Population	6,204,208	974,005
HMB Estimate of Lost	32,007,057	12,627,133
Proportion of Lost/ Population	68.3%	54.8%

Do you see the contrast?

There are twice as many people in the NCS as in the SCS, but there are eight times as many SBC churches and ten times as many SBC members in the SCS. There are as many other Baptist in the SCS with one-half the population as the NCS, and twice as many other Baptists per 1,000 population. There are more other evangelical churches in the NCS, but in ratio to population, the SCS has a three to two ratio of other evangelicals. Over six times as many ethnic people are in the NCS. I believe it has become a common, spontaneous, unofficial goal among NCS leaders that we have as many SBC churches and members in the NCS as in the SCS. The North Central States Missions Thrust will only be a little step in that direction.

USE OF DATA. How have we used this information?

1. Each state has developed its own strategy. There is no organic relationship among the state conventions or between the state conventions and the SBC agencies. Everything has been done on a cooperative, voluntary basis.

2. There has been some cooperative emphasis planning as well as use of common promotional procedures. This has been very low-key.

3. One meeting has been held each year for the training and inspiration of specifically invited leaders from each of the NCS.

4. A combined effort has been made to enlist associational leaders in the planning process and to insure the commitment of the smaller ecclesiastical bodies to the over-all project.

5. Working together, the leaders have been able to pull more resources into the seven-state area and to arouse interest and commitment within the laity. In Illinois, we have raised $1,000,000 in four years for the salaries of pastors of new churches, above and beyond everything else. This has been done by lay task forces in each of the district associations.

INGREDIENTS OF A REGIONAL STRATEGY. To talk directly about a regional strategy, I will have to come back to the strategy of the Illinois Baptist State Association. I would suggest the following twelve steps:

1. Begin with the divine imperative.

2. Build on self-study. Know who you are and what you have been doing.

3. Know your region geographically, culturally, and ecclesiastically. Pinpoint areas where there is evidence of need for new churches.

4. Have clear objectives and specific goals.

5. Determine what factors in an area will dictate immediate priority consideration or continued priority consideration.

6. Identify and make advantageous use of homogeneous units.

7. Identify felt needs as a means of discovering areas of responsiveness.

8. Mobilize missionary staff, volunteers, and financial resources to meet felt needs.

9. Don't permit your missionary strategy or method to be dictated by real estate considerations. Renounce the "temple" complex in church planting.

10. Give central responsibility to volunteers. Let the laity find their gifts and ministries in church extension skills.

11. Make direct evangelism a major factor in your strategy.

12. Count on God to give a marvelous increase. "He gives to His beloved even in his sleep" (Psa. 127:2).

NOTES

[1]See Ezra Earl Jones, *Strategies for New Churches* (New York: Harper and Row Publishers, 1976), p. 101, for a suggestion much like this definition.
[2]See Donald A. McGavran, "Church Growth in America through Planting New Congregations," the closing address of the Consultation on Evangelism and Church Growth, October 1976, Kansas City, MO.
[3]I assume that these two terms that have arisen from the Church Growth Movement do not need definition. If you are not familiar with the four kinds of church growth that have been described in recent years turn to pages eighty-five and eighty-six.

3

Developing a Congregational Strategy for Church Planting

*Church planting
is a task
of the local church.
This is based
on Scripture.
Also,
it is a more practical,
efficient,
and effective way
than any other system.*

F. Jack Redford, 1979

Jack Redford, director of the Division of
Church Extension for Southern Baptists' Home Mission
Board, alleges that "church planting is primarily the task of
a local church." (I agree with him wholeheartedly.) He
insists that beginning new churches is a "normal and
natural function for a church. If it does not take on this
task, it has become root bound."[1]

I have not traced the roots of this missionary
conviction, but it is deeply ingrained in the Southern
Baptist mentality. Historically, it might be traced back
to Subbel Stearns and the Sandy Creek Church of North
Carolina. That church, constituted in 1754, was the first
Separatist Baptist church in the South to survive for any
length of time, and it was the mother church to many
congregations in North Carolina, Virginia, and Georgia in
the eighteenth century. This church and the numerous
churches and associations that were spawned from it
provided much of the spiritual heritage out of which
Southern Baptist evangelistic enthusiasm has grown.[2]

It is my suspicion, however, that the axiom that
"church planting is primarily the task of a local church"
took its substance from Gospel Missionism, the
missionary expression of the Landmark Movement. This
movement, which arose in the 1880s, threatened the

very life of the Convention. Overseas, Gospel Missioners maintained that the missionaries should adopt the living conditions of the people where they served and that churches should be self-controlling and self-supporting from the beginning. In the homeland, the leaders of this movement objected to mission boards and insisted that the local church be the agency through which missionaries were sent and supported.

The Convention rejected Gospel Missionism, but the movement left an indelible mark on Southern Baptist missionary principles, especially in their formulation and application in America.

LOCAL CHURCH DISINTEREST IN CHURCH PLANTING

Whatever may be the historical roots of the axiom among Southern Baptists that missionary responsibility lodges with the local church, that conviction is certainly not one that is shared directly by leaders of most other denominations, nor is it reflected in denominational structures. Church planting, for most of the larger ecclesiastical bodies, is the responsibility of the national church, regional organizations, or home mission agencies.

This conviction is shared by leaders of local churches. In fact, there has been and continues to be an aversion to church planting on the part of many pastors, elders, deacons, and other local church leaders. This is apparent in practice for many Southern Baptist pastors who would, at the same time, defend intellectually and emotionally the principle of local church responsibility in church planting.

Many factors have contributed to this. The first one is related to interdenominational cooperation: *The advocates of ecumenical cooperation have interpreted the multiplication of churches as a denial of the unity of the Church. Church planting is seen as obvious, irrefutable, empirical evidence of the schism of the body.* The multiplication of mono-cultural churches in various geographical areas is viewed as a disgrace, for which we should be ashamed, or a transgression, from which we should turn in repentance.

Admittedly, the duplication of services and ministries has been a costly and confusing situation in overseas missions as well as in this country. For example, Brownwood, Texas, a small central Texas city, was the home for many years of Daniel Baker College (Methodist) and Howard Payne College (Baptist). About eighty miles farther west, in a little larger city — Abilene, Texas — there was McMurray College (Methodist), Hardin Simmons College (Baptist), and Abilene Christian College (Churches of Christ). With the exception of Daniel Baker, which no longer exists as a separate institution, all of these have become universities.

In spite of multiple examples of this kind of evidence, I believe that a monopoly is a dangerous pattern ecclesiastically and evangelistically, as well as commercially and politically. Comity agreements, in time, produce religious monopolies or establishments. At best, they produce a monopolizing attitude and an "establishment" mentality that is more interested in protecting turf and maintaining hegemony than aggressively discipling and developing the various peoples of an area. Comity arrangements often crystallize certain missionary methods that become wooden and unproductive. They can result in an insensitivity to human need and deplete the evangelical passion for souls that should mark biblical Christianity.

A second factor that has produced an aversion to church planting on the part of local church leaders and denominational leaders is related to technology: *Modern transportation has greatly extended the effective radius of strong, exciting churches.* People can travel farther, quicker. There is no need for new congregations, church leaders allege, when large, well-staffed, well-housed, full-programmed churches can be reached with no serious time problems. This whole philosophy is based on the idea, of course, that either the community which a large church serves is a cultural monolith, or that a culturally conglomerate church is the best kind of church and the only kind that should receive high visibility.

At the opposite pole lies a third factor which has contributed to the disinterest in church planting by local church leaders: *Our frightful struggle with racism, Anglo-Saxon ethnocentrism, and the social exclusiveness of middle-class respectability over the past quarter century has idealized conglomerate churches.* Missions and denominational leaders express pride in and give high marks to those churches which have within their fellowship representatives of racial, ethnic, and socio-economic diversity. Evidence of cross-cultural inclusiveness seems much more significant to church leaders than successful evangelistic penetration of the various segments of society. Our denominational reward system, the way we "stroke" pastors and other local church leaders, has actually discouraged church planting.

A fourth factor that has contributed to the disinterest in church planting by the leaders of local churches is also related to the reward system: *Interest in developing mega-churches exists today.* The Church Growth Movement has contributed to the development of this factor ever since it has addressed itself to the American situation. The focus on greatly growing churches, which most often are described after they have become large churches, has contributed to the romance with mega-churches.[3] One would hope that the focus of the Church Growth Movement on church planting in America will eventually bring this into proper balance.

I affirm the growth of large churches. But two or three things need to be emphasized. First, *big churches always come from little churches.* Second, it needs to be said again and again that *success in the numerical growth of a local church does not preclude efforts to get involved in planting daughter churches.* Finally, *the contribution made by small churches needs to be realistically assessed.*

I cannot speak about other denominational groups,

but for Southern Baptists, smaller churches are more
effective in evangelism than are the larger churches. In a
report prepared in May 1978, entitled "A Study of the
Relationship of Church Size and Church Age to Number
of Baptisms and Baptism Rates," Clay Price and Phillip
Jones of the Home Mission Board, SBC, found that "the
younger the church and the smaller the church, the
higher the baptism rate."[4] In fact, in terms of baptisms
in 1976, the statistical year upon which the report was
made, Southern Baptist churches with less than 100
resident members baptized almost two more people per
hundred resident members than those churches with
more than 500 resident members. If the age of churches is
considered, the churches under ten years of age with
less than 100 resident members are almost three times as
effective evangelistically as the churches over forty
years of age with more than 500 resident members. There
is no basis for demeaning the small church when
discussing evangelistic effectiveness.

Many other factors could be mentioned. The reasons
for lack of interest in church planting by the leaders of
local churches are much more complex than I have
described here. However, the question I want to address
is not what holds us back, but what can we do to move
forward to a strategy for church planting in a local church?
To respond to this subject, I want to describe the brief
history of the Berea Baptist Church of Woodridge,
Illinois. Then I want to make a few simple observations
about how a similar multiplication strategy can be
developed in other churches.

BEREA OF WOODRIDGE

Berea Baptist Church is a new congregation in
Woodridge, Illinois. It provides an excellent illustration for
my purpose. It is a church that has a bold strategy for
expansion growth and is located approximately in the
geographic center of five relatively underchurched
Chicago suburbs. This in itself is nothing extraordinary.

But this church also has a bold strategy for extension and bridging growth and has already demonstrated that it can plant daughter churches that experience significant, stable growth, even when planted across cultural barriers.

Frank Radcliff serves as pastor of this congregation. He was converted as an adult and nurtured under the ministry of an excellent and effective Southern Baptist pastor in Texas. He learned well. The church where he served as pastor in Amarillo, Texas, baptized over 300 persons each year during the three years preceding his move to Illinois. He is an excellent preacher, an outstanding motivator, an imaginative leader, and a ceaseless soul-winner.

Soon after his conversion he wanted to return to his home state of West Virginia to develop a Southern Baptist church, but, because of his lack of experience and training, he was turned down by denominational leaders in that state. In 1974 and in 1976, he and his family became convinced that God was leading them to begin a church in one of the great industrial centers of America. They investigated and prayed.

At the same time, the Illinois Baptist State Association was just beginning a church planter program. We decided to attempt to fully fund pastors in several strategic places in the state for a three-year period. We identified a strategic place as one where there were great church planting needs and where a church could serve as a hub from which other churches might be started.

We worked cooperatively with the mission committees of the various local associations of churches. The missions committee of the Chicago Metro Baptist Association had identified Oak Park as one of those key cities in the Chicago area where a church was needed. Pastor Radcliff and several lay leaders from Texas traveled to Chicago to investigate the opportunity there. The lay leaders became so excited that when the decision was made to begin in Oak Park, eleven people from Amarillo decided to move to the area and serve with the Radcliffs. They quit their jobs, closed their

businesses, and moved to the Chicago area and looked
for work.

Before the group arrived, they committed themselves to plant not just one church, but one each year.
They arrived in August 1975. Within six months, a
congregation of more than 100 had been gathered in Oak
Park. It was gathered primarily among lower middle-
class whites, the great neglected group in what has been
for a period of sixty years one of Chicago's most affluent
suburbs.

When the church leaders became convinced that
God was leading them to establish another congregation,
they left the Oak Park church under the leadership of
one of the Texas laymen whom God had called into
the ministry, and the larger group moved to the
southwestern suburb of Woodridge, then a city of about
20,000 with no Baptist or aggressive evangelical church.

During the first forty months of the new church's
existence, ten more people from Amarillo came to
strengthen the work. On their third anniversary this
congregation had over 1,000 in attendance, ordained
Frank Radcliff, Jr., to the ministry, licensed thirteen men
to exercise their gifts in preaching, and had forty-seven
adult professions of faith. They now have 480 resident
members, average over 600 in Sunday school, and own
eight choice acres. Although their buildings are
inadequate, they conduct two Sunday schools, a day care
center, and a parochial school from kindergarten to the
twelfth grade. They want to relocate a short distance
away where they can purchase 200 acres. They hope to
have a campus that will house a Bible college, a children's
camp, a home for alcoholics and drug addicts, and in
general serve as the training center for those who will
help to plant a ring of churches around the city of
Chicago, as well as reach into the inner city. They have
already produced one series of television programs and
plan to use that medium again.

What has this church done about planting daughter
churches? In addition to the Bethany Baptist Church in
Oak Park, the Berea Church has planted a church in

Glendale Heights, a city just north of Wheaton, Illinois. This church is led by a very able and effective member of the second group of workers who came from Amarillo. On its second anniversary, in August 1979, 172 were present. The church was started in the pastor's home, with the five members of his family. It already has an amazing array of need-meeting ministries and could become one of the stronger Southern Baptist churches in the Chicago area within a very few years.

The Berea Church has a significant number of blacks in its membership. However, in their extensive door-to-door visitation program they were told over and over by black parents that they did not wish to attend nor to allow their children to attend a "honky church." Therefore, a new congregation was begun in nearby Bolingbrook, led by a black pastor. After about a year that congregation has more than 100 in attendance.

Hispanic peoples were touched by the ministries of the Berea Church, and the pastor himself began to teach a Bible class on Sunday morning for this group. Last June, a bilingual Hispanic graduate of Southwestern Baptist Theological Seminary was called to become the pastor of this group, and its status was changed from a Spanish department to a Spanish-speaking chapel. There has been a disruption of this fellowship, and the Spanish-speaking pastor and several Spanish-speaking families have withdrawn to organize into an independent church. This occurred before the group had gained adequate strength to function independently. However, the Berea Church has continued its Spanish ministry and expects to have a group gathered within six months that will be large enough to form another chapel.

The Berea Church also served as one of the co-sponsors of a new church in York Center for a short period of time. This young church is now organized as an independent entity. In November 1979, York Center church began gathering a new congregation among the Filipinos in the Chicago area. The Berea Church has already identified at least three more cities where it hopes to plant daughter churches within the immediate future.

The Berea Church has maintained a close working relationship with the Missions Department and the Language Missions Department of the state convention. A fairly extensive subsidy program has helped to fund the pastors' salaries in the daughter churches. Nevertheless, the financial growth of the mother church has been phenomenal. The state convention has put nothing into lands or buildings for the Berea Church.

I do not want to suggest, of course, that the church has no problems. Big, bold plans necessitate large dollar commitments. Sometimes the plans have materialized faster than the supporting dollars. The problem of incorporating, indoctrinating, and training many new Christians has been a serious one. Providing for a larger staff has been a major concern. Enduring the hostility and accusations of fellow pastors who have not experienced significant growth has not always been easy. Many mistakes—the pastor and church leaders will agree—have been made.

OBSERVATIONS ABOUT STRATEGY

However, I am not attempting to offer a critique. I have told this story because I think it suggests some conditions essential to a bold and effective strategy for church planting on the part of a local church. My observations about these essential conditions will not be comprehensive, nor will they necessarily be in proper order.

1. I would stress the importance of a dynamic, creative leader who thinks big, who has a genuine compassion for men without Christ, and an overpowering commitment to obey Jesus Christ in his own life. I doubt that a church will ever develop a deliberate, long-range plan for church planting without a leader who is himself committed to such a strategy.

2. In order for a congregation to develop a strategy for planting churches, that congregation—or, at least its principal leaders—must have assumed evangelistic responsibility for a significant geographical area. The

burden of an entire city or county which needs to know Christ must be embraced. A church planting strategy grows out of this kind of vision and concern. Frank Radcliff, Jr., and the leaders of his church speak, with all sincerity, of winning Chicago to Christ. They have a plan to do it. Their plan does not exclude other Christians. In fact, they rejoice when other churches grow and when new congregations are started by sister churches. But that does not lessen their burden for Chicago.

3. Flexibility is another ingredient that is essential to a church planting strategy. I have not seen a church more flexible in methods than Berea. When they discover a felt need, they attempt to rise to the occasion and meet it. The first priority is to evangelize the area effectively and to incorporate the believers into a thriving congregation. When this requires special purpose congregations, the Berea church is sensitive to this and has sufficient commitment to do it.

4. A transferable philosophy of ministry may be essential to developing an effective, long-range church planting strategy. Thus far, the leadership of the Berea Church seems to have been successful in passing on a philosophy and attitude that desires, expects, and counts on growth. The daughter churches are marked by the same concerns and commitments as Berea. If new churches are to be successfully planted by a mother church, this kind of transferable approach to the growth task could play an important part.

5. The congregation and its leaders need to have a single commitment to direct evangelism done by the laity. This shapes its commitment to church planting and appears as a trait in the daughter churches as well. A bus ministry has played an important part in the growth of the Berea Church and its daughter congregations. But the chief concern of the bus ministry is not how many people ride the buses. Its chief purposes are to give high visibility to the church, to provide a vehicle for knocking on many doors every week, and to provide a training ground for new Christians. Radcliff says that a bus is a "crutch" that the new Christian can use in his first efforts to share his faith.

6. Another essential is an unyielding commitment to the word of God, not only in doctrine, but also in basic strategy along with a firm belief in the direct leadership of the Holy Spirit. These have helped to shape the church planting strategy of the Berea Church. The church sees church planting as a basic New Testament methodology for evangelistic faithfulness. They are more concerned that the Holy Spirit is leading to an area or to a homogeneous group for a new church than they are about the findings of a community survey.

7. A positive, forward-looking attitude that is grounded in a wholesome faith in God is another essential. This is a contributing factor to the congregational strategy of Berea for church planting. The Berea Church has a motto that it seems to live by: "Let's give God a chance." They say this over and over again. Then they set out to do it.

8. A team approach to church planting needs to be fully explored, both by leaders of local churches and denominational strategists. Most denominational approaches to church planting are conceived as beginning with a nucleus of believers. Perhaps, however, the idea of a committed team, a team with a sense of calling from God and a dream that includes more than one new church, needs to be examined. In developing a church planting strategy for a local church, it certainly has merit.

WHAT CAN YOU DO?

Most of us do not picture ourselves as I have described Frank Radcliff, Jr. If you were to meet him, you probably wouldn't think at first that he is the kind of man I have described. Let me suggest several things that you can do if you are a pastor, a lay leader in a congregation, or are a seminarian who plans to become a pastor.

1. *Accept personal evangelistic responsibility for all peoples.* You probably think that I am being melodramatic or that I am asking you to become a megalomaniac. But Paul said in Romans, "I am under obligation both to the

Greeks and Barbarians, both to the wise and to the foolish." In Ephesians 3:8, he said, "To me, the very least of all saints, this grace was given, to preach to the Gentiles the unfathomable riches of Christ." Accept personal responsibility! You probably will not be successful in leading the church you serve to sustain a strategy for church planting if it is not the passion of your own life to reach all peoples that you can with the gospel of Christ.

2. *Think bigger than the boundaries of your own congregation and ways you can extend those boundaries.* Dare to dream of an effective evangelistic strategy for a whole county, an entire city, or an entire urban region. Take a close look at the community where your own church is located. Who are the unchurched people there? How many of them are so distant from your church in terms of culture or socio-economic factors or race that you must do more than use good growth methods to reach them effectively? Ask yourself how many of these you can realistically hope to reach only through a church planting strategy. I doubt that you'll ever lead your church to have an enlarged vision that sees peoples, rather than just individuals, if you do not have that vision yourself.

3. *Ask God for a deep conviction that he wants the lost found and that he wants to use his people to do the job.* I'd like to stress this strongly. All committed Christians would agree with this doctrine, but often — and I struggle with this in my own life — we get so busy doing the "things" of our ministry that we neglect the obligations of the doctrine. We do not nurture this compassion. If you do not have a conviction that is so deep that you cannot get away from it, then ask God to give it to you.

If the most profound justification for church planting that you can identify is the sociological axiom that the church is one of the necessary institutions of society, you are never going to lead a church through a sustained church planting strategy. An evangelistic compassion for those without Jesus Christ must motivate you and your church.

4

Creating a Climate for Planting New Churches

Being a real
New Testament church
means believing
and doing what the
New Testament church did.
It means
planting new churches
as the New Testament church did. . . .
Church multiplication
was an essential part
of New Testament life.

Donald A. McGavran, 1977

In 1776, there were less than 3,000 churches
in America. There are more than 300,000 in 1980.
"Enough is enough!" many people are saying. Some
Christian leaders have been saying that all of this
century. The division of the Christian population into
many local congregations, large and small, is part of the
scandal of modern Christianity, they maintain. "If
anything is true," these people say, "we have too many
churches."

In the last chapter I discussed several factors that have
contributed to the prevailing mental climate that the
time for planting new churches in America has passed.
Let me summarize them.

1. Superior roadways and rapid transportation — both
private and public — have made established meeting
houses accessible to people from distant communities.

2. Our struggle to overcome social, cultural, and racial
segregation within churches has idealized conglomerate
churches and mitigated against starting churches in the
various segments of society.

3. The prevalent infatuation with "giant" churches —
from whatever motivation — has caused many church
leaders to resist the planting of new churches as a threat
to empire.

4. Ecclesiastical détente among American Christians in this century has produced something of a "religious settlement" among the various denominations. It has become unthinkable for Southern Baptists, for example, to consider gathering churches where there are no Southern Baptist prospects. Everyone, this mentality suggests, has some preference. To attempt to win a person to active allegiance to Christ and add him to a congregation different from his preference or different from the one nearest his home is unabashedly called "proselyting" and "sheep stealing."

Given this milieu, is it possible to create a climate for church planting within a congregation? Can a church be prepared for motherhood? How is the apostolate of the New Testament church to be actualized, personalized, and localized in this last quarter of the twentieth century?

I'm not sure that I can answer these questions with any degree of finality. Anything I will say must be considered tentative and temporal. It must be considered tentative because the church leadership may attempt all the things I suggest and still find the church unwilling to commit itself to new work. There are many intangibles we cannot examine for lack of time, and others I cannot analyze for lack of skill. What I say must be considered temporal because churches are subject to change, even though some people despair that certain churches will ever change. What might work now may be ineffectual in five years. I do hope, however, to discuss some principles that are supra-temporal.

THE SPIRITUAL PREPARATION OF THE CHURCH

How do you lay a spiritual foundation for starting new churches in a modern American congregation? What steps can be taken to develop a passion for church planting? I will suggest five.

1. *Set church planting in biblical perspective.* The mission of the church succinctly stated is, I insist, to

proclaim the good news of Jesus Christ in the power of the Holy Spirit among all the social groupings of mankind, and to gather those who respond into churches. Planting churches is at the heart of the apostolate of the church of the New Testament. Planting churches is the essence of the apostolic gift. Evangelicals in America, and in all places during periods of significant growth, have majored on this task. Evangelism (winning to commitment to Christ) is not complete until churches are gathered. In recent years the social establishment of evangelicals has been recognized and we have made rapid strides toward affluence and rock-ribbed respectability. In this situation, we have lost sight of this central biblical perspective. In preaching and teaching, the importance and centrality of church planting needs to be imbedded in the congregation.

2. *Magnify the ministry of the laity.* The task of church planting can never be achieved by, nor should it be conceived as, the labor of clergy. Adequate spiritual preparation should include a clear concept of the significance of the ministry of all the people of God. Men and women in churches are called to meaningful spiritual ministry, not just to menial, "secular" tasks. Biblically and historically it has been the laity, mobilized and motivated to spiritual ministry, which has produced the spontaneous expansion of the church.

3. *Maximize the central place of the Holy Spirit in the mission of the church, and emphasize the necessity and possibility for every believer to be filled and led by the Spirit of God.* The Spirit of God is the Spirit of missions. It is he who is the executor of God's mission to the world in Christ. The purpose of God in redemption, the plan of God for the ages, is to be actualized by the ministry of the Spirit working in and through the Church.

Agreement on the central place of the Spirit is easily secured. Personal, experiential acquaintance with the Holy Spirit's work in the individual Christian's life has been more difficult to find among many evangelicals since the rise of Pentecostalism during the first decade of this century. Nevertheless, adequate spiritual preparation for church planting in a local congregation demands that we teach and preach:

(a) *the necessity for all believers to be filled with and to walk in the Spirit.*

(b) *the need for all Christians to be led by the Spirit in their daily lives and to surrender themselves to God as instruments of righteousness, and then to become productive members of the body of Christ.*

(c) *the responsibility of each believer to attempt to discover the particular gift given him or her by the Spirit, and to exercise this gift so that the church might be built up and continue to grow.*

(d) *that the Holy Spirit empowers the most backward Christian for effective ministry and witness.*[1]

4. *Provide opportunity for periodic renewal.* The need to re-create must be met if a church is to maintain the spiritual dynamic essential to church planting. The body of Christ must be built up, as well as added to. Edification and evangelism are the twin tasks that constantly face the church. Retreats and small groups meeting for Bible study and prayer are two excellent ways to pursue this step; there are many others.

5. *Major on direct evangelism.* Churches grow in only three ways: by baptism of the children of members; by addition of those who transfer from other churches; and by conversions from the world. The first two will never win the world to Christ, but a church which regularly wins men and women to Christ from the world can plant another church which will do the same. Effective and habitual efforts in direct evangelism will also contribute to the spiritual foundation essential to getting a church ready for church planting.

THE MENTAL PREPARATION OF THE CHURCH

How do you develop a mentality for beginning new churches in a contemporary American congregation?

What steps can be taken to create a mental climate for church planting? Several matters deserve attention:

1. *Actualize mission philosophy.* It is amazing how many "missionary" churches are not missionary. They may have a stated policy of missionary concern and have a limited commitment to the financial support of overseas missions, but they never have considered putting their missionary philosophy into action through direct support and personal involvement. The missionary nature of the congregation is only a rumor. One way a local church can be prepared for church planting is to specify the mission philosophy of the church—first in words, and then in concrete challenges. The church should focus on real opportunities for its membership to practice what is preached in missionary terms.

2. *Be realistic about social, cultural, and geographical boundaries.* A congregation—no matter how large—which meets in Hammond, Indiana, cannot adequately minister to Waukegan, Illinois, over 100 miles away, no matter how large the bus or how dedicated the workers. As obvious as that may be, there are hundreds of evangelical churches, mostly Baptist, which are presently attempting that strategy. (Most of them do not do it as effectively as that church in Hammond!)

Cultural and social boundaries are just as real as geographical boundaries. There are conglomerate churches—composed of groupings from various socio-economic, racial, and cultural strata, but these are few, and the men who can gather them together are rare. Most of us do our most effective ministry within certain related pieces of the mosaic of human society. We do not communicate effectively across cultural lines.

This is not a defense of racial segregation, cultural exclusivism, or social snobbery within churches. If a church does not address the gospel to everyone in its community (not just welcome them if they come, but actively evangelize them), it is in danger of vitiating its New Testament character. Refusal to offer Christ aggressively to everyone in a church's community is a mutation of New Testament Christianity just as surely as doctrinal heresy. It is an attempt, however, to underline the facts that people do not like to cross cultural and social barriers to become Christians, that we most readily and effectively witness to our peers, and that churches grow most naturally along these larger-family lines. This principle needs to be recognized as reality, so that the sponsoring church can see the need for planting churches within every segment of human society. It is patently un-Christian to insist, *de facto,* that the only way a garbage man can become a Christian and active church member is in the church where the vice-president of the bank is a principal leader.

3. *Combat local-church myopia.* There is an innate shortsightedness in mankind, a tendency to look at the local, at what is ours, and to focus full energies in that direction. One's own community, no matter how needy, is not the whole world. Believers develop something akin to militant nationalism in reference to their own church. It is extremely rational to many people to say, "Why should we preach the gospel in other places when we have not won our own community as yet?" Such a philosophy would have confined Christianity to Judea and Galilee as an insignificant sect of Judaism.

4. *Be honest about small church efficiency.* We are living in a "big" church era. Church and church staff size have become status symbols. Let me discuss this point, mentioned in the previous chapter, by using some additional data concerning Southern Baptist Convention churches. Huge churches have not historically characterized Southern Baptists. There were only seventeen SBC churches with more than 2,000 members in 1924. By 1940, however, there were more than 100. In 1979, 563 SBC churches had more than 2,000 members, 185 of these counted over 3,000 members.

Small churches are much more efficient in terms of evangelism than large churches in the Southern Baptist Convention. In 1979, for instance, SBC churches between 2,000 and 3,000 in membership averaged fifty-seven baptisms. That same year the churches with memberships of 200-300 averaged seven baptisms. Ten of the smaller churches (200-300) would have baptized thirteen more people than one large church (2,000-3,000). In Illinois, small churches (fifty to ninety-nine members) baptized four each. Larger churches (1,500-1,999 in membership) averaged twenty-three baptisms. Thirty churches with fifty members each would have won to Christ almost 300 percent more people than one church with 1,500 members.[2]

This requires mental toughness in a day of big-church romance. Information like this needs to be shared over and over again with the budding mother church. Don F. Mabrey's study, "The Demand for Dynamic Evangelism," should be required reading for all persons responsible for or interested in church planting, and it would provide good material for helping some denominational executives develop a proper appreciation for "little, mission-type churches."

5. *Develop a congregational strategy for church planting.* Long-range planning has come of age among most Protestants. While churches are setting goals, determining actions, and assigning responsibility for growth in membership, building development, Sunday school attendance, etc., each church should also develop a long-range strategy for church planting over the years.

Evangelical leaders are doing tough thinking about church growth, and a precise language has been developed about the subject. Begin passing this information on to the membership of your congregation. Four kinds of church growth have been identified.[3] I believe that most churches can be involved in all four simultaneously.

Internal growth is growth in grace. Goals should be set and a strategy should be developed to help the church members grow toward Christlikeness and to help them learn how to be led by the Holy Spirit. To focus *only* on this kind of growth is a tragic mistake that leads to holy snobbery and a spiritual ghetto mentality. To do this is a very powerful temptation, especially to those of us who have been shaped by the nineteenth century Holiness Movement. A church can strangle on a total inward focus.

Expansion growth is the numerical increase of the

church within its own community. This is desirable and essential. Most planning will focus on this kind of growth. It is, however, an overweening concern for this kind of growth as the only way a church can grow numerically that hinders church planting among evangelicals today.

Extension growth is that which takes place when a church plants a daughter church among people of the same general homogeneous group as the mother church. This, too, is church growth and is, in fact, the quickest way to turn the growth graph of a local church upward. Extension growth multiplies the church's ministry in a dramatic way. It is the church growing in another locale. It must not be seen as competition. A strategy for extension growth should be developed.

Bridging growth is that which takes place when a church plants a daughter congregation in a radically different cultural, linguistic, or racial community. It might be in another geographical area, or in the same community where the mother church is scattered. It might meet in the same building. Steps should be taken to identify and to plant new churches in these cultural and racial pockets.

6. *Cultivate the spirit of winning.* A positive mental attitude is essential to constant achievement. The church is called to victory, to growth, and to the multiplication of units. A church whose members believe that under God they can, can! One of the most essential factors to proper mental preparation for church planting is a spirit of faith, victory, and confidence permeating the congregation and its leaders. A church that expects great things from God can attempt great things for God.

PREPARING THE CHURCH ORGANIZATIONALLY

How do you devise an organizational foundation for church planting? Can steps be taken to develop a congregational structure for starting new churches? How can this structure contribute to a church extension

climate in the congregation? I will suggest five
guidelines.

1. *Make specific assignments for leadership in
church planting to responsible members of the
congregation.* Select a missions committee, missionary
board, a church extension task force, or form a Paul and
Silas society, an A (Aquila) and P (Priscilla) band, or
local missions module within the congregation. Whatever
form you might choose, place the responsibility for this
significant function of the church on the shoulders of lay
leaders. It is tragic, but true, that in the minds of most
evangelicals in America, Matthew 28:19, 20 has been the
exclusive domain of the overseas mission. At least this
has been characteristic since 1886. This idea has given a
distorted view of the mission of the church to the
average church member. By making missions the sole
responsibility of those especially called and trained for
cross-cultural evangelism and of national and regional
boards and societies, usually in distant cities, churches
as a whole have been robbed of the glory of direct
involvement in the most primary of all mission
tasks — that of gathering new disciples of Christ into new,
growing congregations.

Assigning specific responsibilities to lay leaders will
also counteract a most unscriptural notion that the
responsibility for starting new churches in the American
context belongs to state, regional, and national boards
or societies and is divorced from the essential duties of
churches or individuals.

2. *Give the church planting task force (CPT) status in
the congregation.* It should rank along with the board of
Christian education, the budget and finance committee,
the youth council, etc., as a primary organization in the
administration of the total ministry of the church.

3. *Choose members for the CPT who will provide
creative, forceful leadership.* Too often, all other
leadership positions in the church organizations are
filled first. Then, those positions structured with
responsibility beyond the immediate community of the
church are manned by the unwilling and/or inept.

Persons chosen for the CPT should have a missionary and evangelical passion and a personal faith that is contagious. They should be able and willing to devote time to gathering and analyzing data about community needs. They should command the attention and respect of the congregation when they speak.

4. *Train the CPT for its job.* Begin with bare essentials. Do *not* share all the minute details at a one-and-only training session. Let the CPT begin to function, and then provide continual training opportunities that are dictated by functional needs. This approach vastly increases the relevancy of training information and provides high motivation for training opportunities.

5. *Turn the CPT loose to function.* There are at least five primary functions of a CPT:

   (a) *A prophetic function.* Churches have, since the Jerusalem Church of Acts, tended to become ingrown, exclusive, self-centered, and institutionalized. The CPT, by reminding the church of the biblical mandate and by sharing the needs of communities calls it back to its scriptural purpose.

   (b) *A planning function.* The CPT must develop church extension eyes just as a student pilot must develop navigational eyes. It must be able to recognize evidence of unreached pockets of people. This function is not primarily intuitive. It requires study of census data and housing and economic patterns. Recognition is only the beginning. The CPT must develop strategies to penetrate unreached populations and gather new congregations. The strategies must be communicated to the congregation.

   (c) *A promotion function.* The findings and recommendations of the CPT should be publicized, reported, discussed, and gossiped throughout the entire membership. Do not restrict the reports to the meetings of the congregation. Both need and potential should

be emphasized. The CPT should make a
church planting project as exciting and
pervasive as an every-member financial
canvass, an evangelistic campaign, or a building
program.

(d) *An enlistment function.* Churches have within
their membership individuals and families
who have particular gifts for church planting.
The CPT should in every possible way
attempt to discover people with those gifts and
interests. They should share the church
planting needs and their plans with the
congregation in such a way as to evoke such
gifts that might be latent in individuals.

(e) *An implementation function.* The CPT must
have authority, resources, and initiative to see
that plans are carried out, evaluated, and
reshaped until they prove to be effective.[4]

By these or other similar steps, an organizational
structure can be formalized within a congregation with
responsibility for planting new churches. This structure
can and should become a potent force in creating a climate
for church extension.

PREPARING THE CHURCH PRAGMATICALLY

How do you secure concrete involvement from a
potential sponsoring congregation in the task of beginning
new churches? What steps can be taken to *call for
commitment to church planting?* Commitment should
be secured in at least four areas:

1. *Commitment in terms of prayer.* Undergird the
project with prayer. Prayer must not be viewed as exotic
and mystical, but essential and pragmatic. It is the place
to begin, continue, and end any ministry of witness or
service in the name of Jesus. Specific plans should be
made, and individuals and organizations in the church
should be enlisted for concerted, sustained, and explicit
prayer support for the undertaking.

Practically speaking, the first concrete commitment of

the church should be in a program of persistent and fervent prayer.

2. *Commitment in terms of training.* Equip the congregation with the skills necessary for gathering new churches. Most church training programs — except for some devised in very recent years — have been basically maintenance-oriented. We have produced a host of workers who know how to conduct a business meeting and what is the latest in educational psychology. But we have produced very few who make personal witnessing a way of life, who are always touching others with Christ. In the meantime our training programs have died. A host of lay training organizations which equip laymen for spiritual ministry has arisen outside the churches.

Do an evaluation of *all* the unsalaried leaders in your church. How many exert their principal energy in ministry to those in the church? How many are actually trained and assigned toward ministry in the world? This assessment will reveal the area where there is greatest need.

Provide training for various outreach strategies. Most outreach training has been in only two areas: personal evangelism and bus ministry. We must provide training for other options: Bible study fellowships, evangelistic speaking, coffee fellowships, Bible clubs, various community ministries, etc.

Let me emphasize one thing: This practical training must be tied directly to spiritual preparation. It is impossible to share life-at-its-best if you are not experiencing life-at-its-best. The two must go hand in hand.

Pragmatically, new churches demand relevant training opportunities.

3. *Commitment in terms of money.* Underwrite the project with *necessary* funding. I am not speaking here of total support. I know of churches that have refused to sponsor a new work because they could not buy a site, erect a first unit, and put a full-time seminary graduate on the field. That's not what I am calling for. I know of other churches who will sponsor a new work *only* if it

requires *no* support in terms of money or people. To both extremes I call for the commitment of *necessary* funding.

In funding, priorities need to be established. People are much more important than places. Many new churches have been aborted because no worthy meeting place could be found for rent or because no place could be found to build a building. The best money will be spent on personnel. Halls should be rented only when homes are unavailable or too small. Buildings should be erected only as a last resort.

Pragmatically, new churches demand financial commitment just as other programs demand monetary resources.

4. *Commitment in terms of people.* Ask the church to commit people — individuals and families — to church planting just as it commits people to Bible study organizations, to organizations for missionary education and music, or to social activism.

Southern Baptists have begun many new churches with sponsorship in name only, and I'm sure we will start many more this way. Under such "sponsorship" no people and no dollars are committed. It is much better when a church invests part of its life in a new work by providing at least part of the nucleus in the new community.

"But that will weaken the sponsoring church!" is the first reaction. "All this does is divide a fairly strong church and produce two weak ones!" is another.

The worst way to begin a new work is with a church division. If sponsoring churches could be led to see that a new church *multiplies* their ministry, perhaps this could be overcome. I often say to a pastor, "What would you do if two families in your church were transferred to other cities by their employers?" "We would go on and seek other members." That is just the way the church should look at the investment of people in new churches. Expect and look for others whom God will send to fill their places.

The New Testament pattern in evangelism was not to make many new disciples and leave them unrelated to

other Christians. That is why the local church is of
crucial importance. Nor is the biblical pattern to enlarge
existing churches until their membership numbers in
the thousands. The biblical pattern is to move converts
into new churches, let them meet in homes, and then
multiply the number of such churches. In an analogy of
biological cells and churches, Howard Snyder said,
"Normal growth comes by the division of cells, not by the
unlimited expansion of existing cells. The growth of
individual cells beyond a certain point is pathological."[5]

The only way to increase the ratio of Christians to
population in any nation is to multiply the number of
churches. If evangelicals are to make significant progress
in bringing America to Christ, the number of churches
must be multiplied.

These remarks are from my own background as a
Southern Baptist in Illinois, where very often the
churches nearest the areas of need are least able in terms
of money and personnel to sponsor new churches
adequately. This same thing is not true in many areas of the
nation or for other evangelical groups. But there is still
much reluctance to plant people in new units.

Finally, there can be commitment of personnel on
other than a permanent or semi-permanent basis. Groups
of men, women, and young people can be enlisted for
community events and ministries, for surveys, special
projects, and evangelistic campaigns. Involvement of
the whole church in the project over several years is very
desirable.

Pragmatically, new churches demand the involvement
of people in service and witness.

I have not even touched upon one very fundamental
problem involved in creating a climate for planting new
congregations. I have ostensibly assumed that the pastor
is sympathetic with growth by the multiplication of
churches. This is very often not the case. In fact, he is often
the point of primary resistance. How to deal with the
problem is a crucial matter. Nevertheless, if a pastor is
committed to multiplying churches in every segment of

society, an environment for church planting can usually be brought into existence in a local church.

NOTES

[1]This is an adaptation from Hodges, *A Guide To Church Planting* (Chicago: Moody Press, 1973), p. 27.
[2]See *The Quarterly Review* (July-September, 1980), p. 24.
[3]I have used the terminology used by the School of World Missions, Fuller Theological Seminary, because I think it is essential that we use terminology with a precise definition.
[4]The most comprehensive training manual for a CPT, that I have seen, is Division of Mission-Ministries, *The Church Missions Committee Manual* (Atlanta: Home Mission Board, SBC, 1976). See also their very excellent publication for developing a local associational mission strategy, *The Associational Missions Committee Manual* (Atlanta: Home Mission Board, SBC, 1975). I have adapted material from these documents in this section.
[5]Howard A. Snyder, "The Church as God's Agent in Evangelism," in *Let the Earth Hear His Voice,* J. D. Douglas, ed. (Minneapolis, MN: World Wide Publications, 1975), pp. 332, 333.

5

Spontaneous Church Planting in the Inner City

One of the strange,
weird, perplexing,
and paradoxical miracles
of history
is the origin
of the black church
on the North American
continent.

W. J. Hodge, 1972

will turn our attention in this chapter. What I am going
to share is not the result of careful research, but of rather
careful observation in one of the great industrial states
of America and in the nation's third largest city. These
observations will describe the situation in most
northern and western cities, and probably will not be too
far away from that of cities of the South and Southwest.

PURPOSE OF THIS STUDY

I hope to accomplish four things with this investigation.
First, I hope to stimulate further interest in a relatively new
field of American church growth research, one from
which I am convinced we have a great deal to learn.

There are several reasons why so little has been done
in this area. Most of those people passionately interested in
how and why American churches grow or do not grow
have been white themselves and leaders of predominately
white churches, denominations, missions, or educational agencies. During the same period that the Church
Growth Movement has become a reality, most prominent
black church leaders have been committed to problems of
racial and social justice in this country. Church growth
has taken place, I think, and church planting has
continued, but it has not received major emphasis or
paramount attention. In fact, some principles of church
growth have been extremely threatening to men who
have been committed to integration, equality, and justice.

Another problem, of course, is the dearth of reliable
statistics for black churches, and especially for black
Baptist churches. The National Baptist denominational
groups were not included in the Glenmary study of
American churches and church membership in the
middle seventies because the most reliable figures for
numbers of churches and members were only estimates.[2]
Still, the research needs to be done. I doubt that there
were fully reliable statistics for Pentecostals in Latin
America in the sixties. Nevertheless, it is remarkable
what was discovered about the growth of churches when
huge investments of man-hours were devoted to that

The proliferation of Pentecostal congregations is the greatest global church planting story in the twentieth century. There were no Pentecostal holiness churches (I do not speak, of course, of *the* Pentecostal Holiness Church) on January 1, 1901. When one looks at the rise of Pentecostal churches around the world in less than eighty years, he is astounded. In terms of sheer numbers and the relatively successful penetration of just about every "ethclass"[1] in the United States, the multiplication of Pentecostal churches is a most impressive church planting success story.

This story has received a great deal of notice from church growth and mission researchers, and that recognition is justified. Other Christians have much to learn from what God has done through Pentecostal people in the last eight decades. However, there is a second story that has been almost totally overlooked — the rise and growth of black churches, especially black Baptist churches. Students of church growth and practitioners of church extension have hardly stopped to take more than a passing glance at what has been accomplished by these people.

The most dramatic rise and growth of black churches has occurred in the great industrial and commercial centers of America during this century. To this subject we research. This same commitment of man-hours and money will have to be made in order to discover how church growth has occurred in the American black community.

Further, someone needs to discover for us what kind of growth has actually taken place. There can be no doubt that the rise of black Baptists in American industrial centers is a great church planting story. However, whether there has been significant growth of the Body of Jesus Christ in the whole process has not been established. From 1915 to 1930, a great migratory flood took place. It consisted of "the movement of members of the Negro population from rural to urban centers and from the urban South to the urban North."[3] The process began again with the outbreak of World War II and did not abate until the Nixon recession of the early seventies.

Much of the growth of black churches has been biological and transfer growth. We have no way of knowing or judging how well these new black congregations have done in penetrating the pagan pools within the black community. We may have a salient illustration of how big churches — as well as many small churches — come from small rural churches. This in no way detracts from the achievements of those stalwarts of the gospel of Christ, who have produced thousands of churches that now exist in the inner cities of America. They have done this in spite of hardships, lack of monetary assistance, and scant academic or theological training. The story begs for a full and thorough examination in every city.

The second thing I hope to accomplish with this investigation is to call attention to those countless men who have been God's instruments in accomplishing tremendous feats in church planting. They are unknown to nearly all church historians, to denominational and mission executives, and to church growth and church extension leaders. While church historians have been writing about the demise of Protestantism in the inner cities, these men have been gathering the new populations of those cities into Protestant churches. While

denominational and mission executives have been
spending thousands of dollars trying to keep the doors
of church buildings open (in communities from which the
churches that once met in the buildings have long since
departed) and have been going through all kinds of
contortions to hang on to inner city real estate, these
men have been planting churches without the benefit of
real estate, endowments, or mission dollars. While
church extension and church growth specialists have
focused on the declining membership of great old rich
ecclesiastical institutions and on the people who have
moved out, and while they have tried to solve the
problems of prejudice, paternalism, and property, these
men have focused on the newcomers. These newcomers
are the future of these transitional communities. They
are uprooted and are looking for a fellowship where they
can be who they are and where they can worship God the
Father and encounter Christ the Son among their peers.

These church planters have been inconspicuous and
ignored. They may have been highly articulate among
their peers, but considered inarticulate by those who
have overlooked them. Leaders from the Protestant
establishment have talked about the Christlike sacrifice
of those who have commuted from the suburbs to keep
the churches open. These church planters have lived in
the ghettos and the transitional communities, have
identified with the people, and have, in fact, been *of* the
peoples there. They have worked by day or night to make
their own living while these new churches were being
started. "People blindness" expresses itself in many
different ways, and Protestant leaders have overlooked
these church planters.

Third, I hope this discussion will prepare the way for
church leaders to consider another option for dealing with
communities in transition. Very often, church planners
focus upon the transitional churches as institutions rather
than as people. They are concerned with how to
guarantee survival of the institution, rather than how most
effectively to evangelize and to congregationalize the
new peoples who are coming into the community, and
how most effectively to conserve those for Christ and

his Church who have moved from the changing communities. I will go into this in more detail from the perspective of the community in transition in the following chapter. Here, however, I want to suggest church planting in transitional communities as a viable, purposeful way to be faithful to Christ.

Fourth, I hope the material presented here will stimulate an aggressive strategy of church multiplication on the part of black leaders and congregations. What has been achieved is significant, but these leaders agree that in most cases it could have been done more easily and efficiently.

METHOD OF THE STUDY

My method will be very simple. First, I will set the story in historical perspective and look briefly at the growth of black Baptist churches over the last century, especially as this growth has developed in Chicago. I will then expose the church planting methods that were used, or at least the methods being used today. This will be done by introducing five pastors who have planted black Baptist churches in Chicago during the past fifteen years. These churches all happen to be a part of the Southern Baptist Convention, and I have had close association and contact with them over several years. You will get a good picture of what I mean when I speak of "spontaneous church planting in the inner city" as you meet these men. Several reflections will need to be made about what we discover. Finally, I want to challenge leaders of predominantly black churches. I want to call them to deliberate, planned church planting in the decades ahead as a major strategy for bringing America to the feet of Jesus.

HISTORICAL DEVELOPMENTS OF BLACK BAPTISTS

First, we will look at black Baptist churches from a statistical and historical perspective.

When the Southern Baptist Convention was

organized in 1845, there were, it has been alleged, more
blacks in the membership of those churches than
whites.[4] Twenty years later, however, the Civil War was
over, and the process of organizing black Baptist
churches with black leadership swelled to a flood stage. By
1890 there were 12,856 black Baptist churches, with
1,350,000 members, and at the same time the U.S. Bureau
of Census found that there were 17,209 Southern
Baptist Churches with only 1,280,000 members. Ninety
percent of all the black Christians were in twelve
southern states in 1890. This means, of course, that black
Baptists and Southern Baptists essentially occupied the
same territory. By 1906, both groups had made significant
gains. That year the Bureau of Census found that
Southern Baptists had added 4,866 congregations since
1890, so they were up to 21,075 churches and slightly
over 2,000,000 members. The National Baptist Convention
had been formed in 1894 with 18,534 affiliated
churches. When you add black Free Will Baptists and
black Primitive Baptists, the total of black Baptist
churches was 19,582, an increase of more than 6,000
congregations between 1890 and 1906. Total membership reached 2,311,000. Again, 87 percent of the black
church members were in the twelve Southern states.[5] (See
graphs 1 and 2.)

When the U.S. Government took its next census of
religious bodies in 1916, there were 21,213 black Baptist
churches, with a total membership approaching
2,900,000. The great population shift from the rural South
to the urban North continued at full flood, except for
the years during the Great Depression, until shortly after
1970.

In 1899, only five black churches were reported in
Chicago, although the black population was near 30,000.
In 1920, the Chicago Commission on Race Relations
made a very careful study of the Chicago black community.
It received the assignment as a response to the great
race riot of 1919, and the commissioners reported that
there were nineteen "regular" Baptist churches in the
city (congregations occupying more or less permanent

GRAPH 1. **Number of Churches: All black Baptist Churches and Southern Baptist Convention Churches**

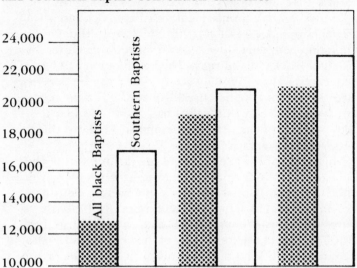

GRAPH 2. **Total Membership: All black Baptist Churches and Southern Baptist Convention Churches**

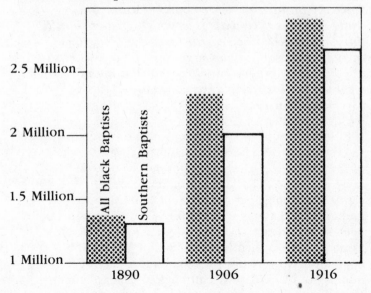

church-type buildings) and sixty-seven storefront
churches, a total of only eighty-six Baptist congregations
among a population of 109,000.[6] In 1940, although
migration had been slowed down for ten years, there were
278,000 blacks in Chicago's black comunity. When
Drake and Caton (1940) were finishing the book *Black
Metropolis,* they found that "Bronzeville" (their term
for the black belt in Chicago) had about 250 black
churches with over 135,000 members.[7] I believe this to
be a very conservative figure.

This pattern was general in all the major cities of the
industrial North during this period. In 1916, there were
only 127 black Baptist churches in Chicago, Detroit,
Cincinnati, Philadelphia, and Baltimore. By 1936, the
Bureau of Census counted 319 churches in those five
cities.[8] However, the reliability of the census figures should
be questioned. Mays and Nicholson (1933), who wrote
an excellent book, *The Negro's Church,* in the early
thirties, used the Federal Census of Religious Bodies for
1926. They had their own research team. They reported:

*Since the number of Negro churches located during this
study by a street canvass is so much greater than the
number given in the Federal Census of Religious Bodies
in 1926, it is safe to conclude that the census reports
are probably too conservative and that many churches
recorded in this study were not reported to the
government in 1926.*[9]

If Chicago is typical of other cities, and if we are willing
to take storefront churches seriously, current estimates
of the number of churches continue to be low.

By 1950, the Black population had grown to 492,000.
By 1970, the black community in Cook County has
multiplied 2.3 times to 1,183,000. The migration has
been so significant that there were more blacks in Cook
County in 1970 than in Alabama and Mississippi
combined. No one has the exact figures about the
number of black Baptist churches in Chicago today.
Counting "regular," storefront, and house churches,

probably there are close to 1,750 black Baptist
churches, with 350,000 members. Multiply this kind of
pattern by all the American cities where there are large
black communities — especially black communities that
have developed since 1945 — and you'll have a picture of
the accomplishment in church planting that has taken
place.

CHURCH PLANTING METHODS

In 1972, when the Illinois Baptist State Association
began to take a hard statistical look at Illinois, we were
face to face with a community of 1.4 million to whom
we as a denomination had never addressed the gospel. We
had made loud claims about preaching the gospel to the
whole state. We had a magnificent rhetoric, but we had
totally ignored the black community in Illinois. In
reality, we have done very little since. As a denomination
we have, I believe, consciously accepted responsibility
to assist in starting and developing Baptist churches among
these peoples as well as others in the state. We have
adopted a long-range strategy for the black community
that we are taking seriously. For the past several years we
have had a number of fully salaried church planters over
the state. Three of the church planters that we have today
are blacks who are attempting to plant churches in
under-churched black communities. We make no effort to
encourage churches aligned with National Baptist
Conventions to affiliate with us. A few do. Most of the
black churches affiliated with the Southern Baptist
Convention in the Metro East St. Louis area hold dual
alignment. Very few are dually aligned in the Chicago area.
We now have fifty black churches across the state, and we
expect to have 100 by 1985.

Where will they come from? Very few of them will be
started by fully salaried church planters. Most of the
growth will come from newly organized, unaligned
churches that are being formed in new black
communities or among the new residents of black

communities in transition. We usually think of
transitional communities only as black to white, or white
to black, but there is a continuous wave of transition
that is black to black, as well.

These congregations will start in homes and will
graduate to storefront churches. In a few years, they will
acquire more church-type buildings and affiliate with
one of our local associations of churches. They will seek
affiliation because of a desperate need for community,
for organizational and educational know-how, and some
because of a hope of realizing some monetary assistance,
probably in terms of building loans. These churches will
arise much like the five I'm about to describe to you,
along with the five remarkable men who began them.

I will start with *Claude Tears*. He is pastor of the First
Corinthians Baptist Church, south of 113th Street, on
State Street. Claude is a tremendous singer. He is the
chief singer in his church and his wife is a fantastic
organist. He came to Chicago from Tennessee in his
teenage years, part of the post World War II migratory
pattern. His wife was born in Chicago. Claude was very
much involved in the music program of a large black
church in Chicago when God called him to preach. In
order to get to church he drove through a changing
community where new young black families were
moving in. He became convinced that God was calling him
to that community. He, his wife, and two other families
began meeting there in July, 1966. When they first started
having Sunday services, they rented a school building;
then they purchased a former supermarket building. They
affiliated with the Southern Baptist Convention in 1972.
In 1973, they purchased a very substantial building with
considerable educational space and a pastor's home.
Their auditorium will seat about 500. They did not get any
assistance from Southern Baptists for the purchase of
the property. They have a radio ministry, a bus ministry,
and a fantastic ministry of witness and service on the
streets of their community. They now have more than
1,200 members, and have more than 1,000 in attendance
on special days. The First Corinthians Baptist Church is

one of the largest Southern Baptist churches in Illinois.

The second man I want you to meet is *Don Sharp.* He is pastor of Faith Tabernacle Missionary Baptist Church, on South Cornell in Chicago. He began to hold weekly Bible studies in the homes of friends in 1964. The fellowship was so good that somebody said, "Why don't we start a church?" He talked with his pastor about it and received a somewhat reluctant permission. In August, the group organized into a church with twelve members. Don said, "Nobody helped us. We didn't begin with mission status. Boom! We were just a church — sink or swim." For five years they met in what had been a warehouse. Then they began to rent space from Cornell Avenue Baptist Church — a church that had previously been named the First Southern Baptist Church of Chicago. Faith Tabernacle began its worship service at noon. Later, the two Sunday schools were combined. Still later, Cornell Avenue Baptist Church relocated in the Hyde Park community, and Faith Tabernacle purchased the church building. The growth of the church has been fairly slow, but very stable. They average about 250 per week in attendance.

Next, I want to introduce you to *Abraham Picou.* He grew up in New Orleans and went to work for Walgreens as a boy. He was transferred by the company to Chicago in 1960, as Walgreens deliberately began to develop stores in the black community. He didn't come looking for work. He was so valuable that his company sent him to Chicago to help in the marketing process in Chicago's black community. Soon he was sent to Cincinnati. He opened the first black Walgreens store outside the city of Chicago. In 1967, the company transferred him back to Chicago to the corporate offices. A Baptist preacher working as the porter in his office, witnessed to him regularly. Picou was eventually led to Christ through his custodian's witness. Picou started attending the church this man served as pastor. In 1968, Abraham Picou was called into the ministry — called to preach. That was very threatening to his pastor, so Picou moved to another church, the Antioch Missionary Baptist Church, and was

there about a year when the pastor left. The Antioch
Church then called him as pastor. At that time, the church
was sixteen years old, but it had only twenty-five
members. It now has 275 members. Picou gave up his
management job and took a $350 monthly cut in salary
to take a five-day-a week job so that he could continue to
serve as pastor of the church.

The fourth man is *Joseph Rainey,* pastor of Christian
Fellowship Missionary Baptist Church. He moved to
Chicago from Tennessee in 1956. He has worked for the
Post Office in Tennessee and Chicago for a total of
twenty-eight years. He served as deacon and Sunday
school superintendent in a Chicago church, and he
helped plant the Haven of Rest Baptist Church in
Chicago. He was called to preach in 1970. When he told his
pastor, the pastor was greatly disturbed. He finally did
consent to let him preach the following November; but
then his pastor suggested that he start holding worship
services in the basement of his home. He began to do that
but soon needed more space. This new congregation
had a great struggle getting a place to meet. When city
inspectors refused to permit the use of a storefront
building for worship services, the church defied the ruling.
Rainey was threatened with jail. The church was locked
out by the Chicago police. In 1976, they finally secured a
permanent building. Now they have about 250
members.

Finally, I want to introduce you to *Eugene Gibson.* He
is pastor of the Mission of Faith Baptist Church. Gibson
worked for a number of years for Spiegel, Inc., in
management. He was bumped when Spiegel merged with a
larger company and he went to work for Chicago City
College to develop a job survival curriculum for that
school. Although he was pastor of a church, he didn't
feel that he was accomplishing much. Then he was struck
down by a heart attack which required a triple bypass
operation. During convalescence he felt a call from God to
develop a black church that would be, as he says, "based
on faith and a strong Bible teaching program." The Bible
teaching program in black Baptist churches has typically

been weak and the black pastors are very concerned
about this. After Gibson's convalescence, he resigned as
pastor and started a new church in a funeral home.
Fantastic things have happened for that congregation
during the two years since it began. This middle-class
black church has acquired a beautiful building without
assistance from the denomination, and they have gathered
250 members. This is a very aggressive young church.

OBSERVATIONS

Let me make some observations about the personal
stories of these men and the churches they have
developed.

1. For most of the black Baptist pastors that I know, and
these in particular, the call to preach is a very
objective — as opposed to a subjective — experience.
Joseph Rainey, for example, was in Los Angeles on
vacation. He had been struggling with an inner call to
preach. He and his wife attended a Church of God in
Christ worship service, and the pastor of that church
walked down to him — a stranger — and said, "God has
called you to preach and prepare the way for you to do it.
What are you waiting for?" When he went back home, he
told his pastor, announced his call publicly, and was soon
preaching in his own home.

2. For these men, to be called to preach is tantamount
to being called to gather a congregation. Black pastors
are not usually comfortable with having another preacher
in the church. To be able to gather a congregation is the
seal of one's call. Thus, planting churches has been
spontaneous rather than planned.

3. Founding pastors plant and serve their churches for
several years with little or no remuneration. For the first
five years the pastor usually puts his own money into the
church and its program at a much higher rate than he
receives in return. Joseph Rainey has been the pastor of his
church for eight years. He has yet to receive one penny
in salary.

4. All of these congregations were started in new black

communities with young families. These communities, from the point of view of whites, were in transition and decline. Much of the present discussion about transitional communities is an expression of cultural chauvinism. It issues from the viewpoint of the people in flight, rather than from the newcomers.

5. The story of these churches is usually an incredible struggle to get property, to get adequate facilities. This struggle and the kind of permanent buildings they get shape the character and personality of the church.

6. Planting a church is always a great step of faith, a bold act of obedience. It is an opportunity to see God at work. It's like crossing the Red Sea—something the congregation continually looks back to and usually celebrates each year.

7. The church is usually established on some spiritual axiom or watchword. At First Corinthians, the people's bedrock principle is "There's nothing too hard for God." They keep pounding away at that idea, proving that it's true.

8. Without exception, these new churches came about as a result of a God-given vision. The vision is most often in the form of a mental and emotional conviction that God wants to build a church in a certain place on certain principles. Sometimes, however, the preacher passes through a mystical encounter with Christ and emerges with a flint-hard conviction that God will accomplish the raising up of a church if he will only be faithful in hardship. Gene Gibson received such a vision while he was in the hospital recovering from heart surgery. When he delayed, hoping to bring the church that he served as pastor up to the new principles on which he felt called to found the church, he says that the Lord spoke to him again. It happened to him at the stroke of midnight, on New Year's Eve, while he was praying as the old year passed. He said, "The Lord spoke to me almost audibly, saying 'Gibson, when are you going to do what I told you to do?'" So, he got up from his knees, went home, called his wife in Philadelphia, and told her he was going to resign as pastor of the old

church and build a new church founded on faith and sound Bible teaching. He did that immediately.

9. These new churches, and the majority of black Baptist churches, develop along larger family lines. Don Sharp says that very often his church penetrates a family through children. The children come, they get involved, and then the mother decides she should be where her child is. The mother will become a member—and maybe the father will begin to attend—and then the mother's sister will come, and then the sister's husband. Perhaps he'll become a deacon, and then they'll get the nieces and nephews. The growth goes on and on, along larger family lines.

The next four observations are not as directly related to these five men as the previous ones were, but they represent significant truth for inner city church planting.

10. The most responsive people to the gospel are generally those who are recently uprooted and who are attempting to get started in a new area. This period of responsiveness does not last forever. It has its limits, and we need to have the most effective evangelistic strategy possible for a changing community during that period of time. New black churches are most often brought to birth in new black communities.

11. Contrary to the opinion of most whites, the black community is not a social monolith. Like the white community, it is a mosaic of many pieces. There are southerners and northerners, rich and poor, middle-class and lower-class, educated and uneducated, working and professional classes. Any strategy for church planting must take the cultural and social pattern of the community into consideration. Denominational leaders, white and black, need to develop an entirely different attitude toward new black church development in the inner city, an attitude instructed by this truth. It plays a big part in the way these new churches get underway.

12. Denominational executives, church planners, and church growth specialists need to be taught by these black church planters. What they have been doing in

the inner city is far superior to what white Protestants have been doing. We have a lot more to learn from those who are building churches in the inner city than from those who are dismantling churches there. Someone needs to develop a major research project to study the growth of the Church in the black communities of great American cities. Much of what I say is only conjecture. I hope students of church growth, white and black, will explore this whole church-growth galaxy.

13. From the point of view of the growth of black Southern Baptist churches, a word needs to be said. In the Chicago area, these churches, almost without exception, are experiencing significant membership growth. The number of churches is also increasing. Many of them seem to be making a wholesome adaptation of SBC organizational methods while retaining the spontaneous, celebrative character of black worship. This, too, deserves study.

TO LEADERS OF BLACK CHURCHES

Since I first began exploring this subject and sharing my observations with others, I have had a number of opportunities to speak specifically with leaders of predominantly black churches, both individually and in groups. What implications does this wonderful story of achievement have for black churches today? Much could be said. Here I will make only three suggestions.

First, take a realistic look at all *the community where your church is located.* Culturally, black churches have not been parish-oriented but pastor-oriented. Nevertheless, God surely holds us especially accountable for those people immediately around us.

Black church members and leaders have been very sensitive to social needs in communities and have become increasingly involved with political structures and community organizations in efforts to effect change. Pastors and other leaders, no matter where they live, have tended to become involved in the community where church planting within the community where the black church exists. Most existing black communities in America have an abundance of churches. I have counted as many as ten storefront churches on both sides of the street in one block of Roosevelt Road in Chicago. However, these churches address themselves to the various sub-cultures of the black community. The day has come, I believe, for vibrant black churches to see the ethnic diversity that is around them and to begin intentionally to engage in cross-cultural church planting in their own immediate communities.

Second, be alert to new black communities that are being formed in our major cities and their suburbs and deliberately and enthusiastically plant new churches in those places.

Communities in transition will have new churches. The growing black populace of many suburbs will have predominately black churches with black leaders. The spontaneous methods that have been used to generate black churches during this century have been effective but painful. They have been painful both in terms of strained relationships and in terms of the difficulty of getting started without aid from a mother church. Much stronger churches more strategically located could have been formed had there been planning and intentional efforts to sponsor and support new congregations.

There is no reason for the same pattern to continue with *all* of its hardships. Those methods that have proven effective but emotionally costly can be improved. Improvement can take place if leaders of black churches will be alert to areas where new black churches are needed and lead their churches to multiply themselves in these new communities through daughter churches.

Third, commit yourselves to plant the vigorous faith and vitality of black churches among all the people-groups that make up America. This is a challenge to cross-cultural evangelism and church planting in the American context.

In most discussions about Christianity and the

the church building is located. This is commendable, and has, in my opinion, contributed to the growth of black churches during the last quarter century. Historians will undoubtedly record that the most important contribution of Christianity to American life in the twentieth century has been the leadership given by black churches to the civil rights movement and the social revolution that was its aftermath.

However, black churches generally need to take a hard look at their community in reference to its ethnic and socio-economic character. In many predominantly black communities the racial and cultural mix is considerable. This cultural pluralism is always a fact in those communities in process of transition.

For purposes of illustration, let me describe an imaginary community where the population is 65 percent black. Thirty-five percent of the population is divided primarily into three other people-groups. Fifteen percent of the population is older whites, a declining number. A growing Hispanic community composes another 14 percent of the total. A small Southeast Asian community, mostly ethnic Chinese, makes up 4 percent of the population. Many other small groups equal about 2 percent of the populace. This kind of racial mix can be found in many black communities in our larger cities.

Furthermore, the black community itself is a conglomeration of very distinct sub-groups. These would range from a number of "Afro-philes," those who have so idealized African roots as to totally reject Christianity as a denial of blackness, to a small group of "Afro-Saxons," those so assimilated with white, middle-class culture as to be uncomfortable within the typical black church. Among these various sub-groups would be a community of French-speaking Haitians. The largest group by far, however, would be those black Americans who can easily be evangelized by existing bla churches.

Taking this kind of look at one's community will enabl leaders of black churches to see the need for and possibility of cross-cultural ministries and cross-cultur

American city, and always in dialogues about missionary strategy for the city, the focus is on designing a plan to get the resources of the suburbs to the central cities. There is a need and place for that concern. However, I am more concerned about transmitting spiritual vitality than I am about sharing material resources and learned leadership skills. Churches with spiritual vitality are needed among all the people-groups of the American population.

Spiritual vitality is present within thousands of black churches. Recent research has shown that blacks are more likely to be evangelicals than whites. Overall, blacks make up about 10 percent of the population but 15 percent of the evangelicals. Nor does evangelical Christianity reside mostly in the suburbs. Actually, suburbs, with only 16 percent of the evangelicals and 27 percent of the populace, are less evangelical than the nonmetropolitan cities, small towns, rural areas, and *inner cities* of this nation. The central cities of America, alleged by many to be barren deserts as far as evangelical Christianity is concerned, have about one-third of the nation's total population. They also have one-third of America's evangelicals.[10] A principle reason for this is the tremendous achievement in evangelism and church planting carried on by black churches and black church leaders throughout this century.

Black churches have yet to awaken to their responsibility to communicate the gospel to white, English-speaking communities or to other language-culture groups. Given the vitality that is within black evangelical Christianity this responsibility shouts for recognition and response. If someone objects that such missionary action is impossible because the black Christian community lacks the resources to evangelize and congregationalize among peoples materially richer than themselves, I respond that in the first century the gospel was habitually passed from the "have-nots" to the "haves." I suggest that black churches adopt the model of the first century churches in modern America.

NOTES

[1]See C. Peter Wagner, *Our Kind of People* (Atlanta: John Knox Press, 1979), pp. 61-74 for a full definition and discussion of this term.

[2]See Paul R. Picard and Bernard Quinn, *Churches and Church Membership in the United States: 1971* (Washington, DC: Glenmary Research Center, 1974).

[3]Benjamin E. Mays and Joseph W. Nicholson, *The Negro's Church* (New York: Russell and Russell, 1933), p. 33.

[4]Edward L. Wheeler, "Understanding and Relating to the Black Community," in B. Carlisle Driggers, compiler, *Churches in Racially Changing Communities,* mimeographed proceedings of the National Leadership Conference, Department of Cooperative Ministries with National Baptists, Home Mission Board, Southern Baptist Convention, Atlanta, GA, 1978, p. 180.

[5]See U.S. Bureau of Census, *Census of Religious Bodies,* 1906, pp. 10 ff., as the source of this information.

[6]Chicago Commission on Race Relations, *The Negro in Chicago* (Chicago: University of Chicago Press, 1922), pp. 142 ff.

[7]St. Clair Drake and Horace R. Cayton, *Black Metropolis* (New York: Harcourt, Brace and Company, 1962), pp. 416 ff.

[8]U.S. Bureau of Census, *Religious Bodies: 1936 Selected Statistics,* Table 1; pp. 16 ff. See also Mays and Nicholson, *op. cit.,* p. 96.

[9]Mays and Nicholson, *ibid.,* p. 97.

[10]*Christianity Today,* December 21, 1979, p. 18.

6

Church Planting: An Untried Option in Urban Transitional Communities

*Metropolitan
transitional areas
should become
mission fields
in the same way
other under-churched areas
of the country
are considered
mission fields.*

George W. Bullard, Jr., 1976

Dilemmas and frustrations are a way of life
for most churches in communities in transition.[1] They
have often been described. No other single concern has
consumed as much time for church and denominational
planners over the past quarter century.

Transitional communities are likely to continue to
make inordinate time demands. Heretofore the general
assumption has been that transitional communities
were in the inner cities and consisted primarily of ethnic
and racial change. Indeed this chapter essentially
discusses the transitional community from that point of
view. But the assumption is no longer completely valid.
Transitional communities can be found in all parts of the
city (or nation for that matter) and the nature of the
change experienced varies over a wide range of social
characteristics.

Central city areas will continue to be a major port of
entry for refugees and immigrants, but may not continue
to be so for migrants from nonmetropolitan areas of the
country. The suburbs may constitute the major
transitional areas in the future, but for now the inner city
remains the most obvious transitional area. Principles
enunciated here should apply to any type of transitional
community.

Tied up with this problem in the central city is a wide range of ethical issues, from "sheep stealing" to racial injustice. Furthermore, the pride, stability, and strength of whole denominations are threatened by the problem. The great prestigious churches in the cities, the bastions of the Protestant hegemony of the past, have been depleted and defeated, and hundreds have died. Many more will die in the future. This demise of great city churches has been one of the factors contributing to the severe decline of world mission giving among many Protestant groups.

As yet no ultimate solution to the problem has been found. As was indicated in the last chapter, in terms of the growth of the Body of Christ, the problem is not really as serious as many have suggested. A recent Gallup survey has shown that the inner cities of America have a greater proportion of evangelicals to population than do the suburbs of our large cities.[2] Where many churches have died, many more have been planted.

One way of meeting the need has hardly been explored by those who do research and spend time deliberately attempting to build strategies for transitional communities.[3] *Along with other strategies* we need to develop plans to plant churches among some of the new peoples in transitional communities.

THE SCENARIO AND ITS OPTIONS

Before addressing this subject directly, let me outline the constellation of factors that produces the multi-sided problem which church leaders usually face in transitional communities.

The church leader finds himself serving a congregation which is, in the main, not a part of the community where its building is located. Many of these members have moved away from the building, but some have never lived in the area. The pastor and other staff members are likely to be in this latter group. The congregation was originally composed of one socio-cultural group, and this character is still obvious in the congregation, especially in the key leadership positions.

The building in which the church meets is often old, expensive to maintain, energy-inefficient, ill-suited to present-day congregational needs, and almost impossible to renovate or remodel.

Most of the membership of the church—especially the leadership, including the pastor—is in a socio-economic group that is significantly different from the people living near the building.

Attendance, membership, and financial support have been in decline for several years. This decline probably began well before the present pastor and staff came on the scene. They inherited a set of problems already in existence.

The general expectation, however, from both the congregation and the denomination, is that the pastor and staff should produce a successful and effective church. "Successful and effective" usually means (1) that the church is solvent, (2) that it is able to contribute fairly significantly to the denomination's missionary and benevolent programs, and (3) that the congregation is growing in numbers.

Given this definition of "successful and effective," the pastor and staff must choose between (1) giving primary consideration to the commuters who, at considerable sacrifice and with commendable dedication, continue to man and support the church's organizations and ministries, or (2) giving primary attention to evangelism and to ministries aimed at people in the immediate community where the church meets for worship. A salient dilemma arises here. Should the pastor (and to a lesser degree, the staff) spend most of his time with those who provide leadership and financial support or with the people in the immediate community of the church building? Whatever option is exercised, the church will fail to be "successful and effective."

The question of programming provides another dilemma for pastor and staff. Should the programs of the church be designed for the stalwart commuters or for

people near the church building? The roles of pastor and
staff are made more difficult by the fact that there often is
a conflict between their views about the church and its
mission and that of many members of the congregation. To
their amazement also, they often find that prejudice,
distrust, and bigotry are just as ingrained in the people
who have moved into the community as among those
who have fled because of change or who remain out of
necessity.

The situation is further complicated by problems of
relationship and understanding. The pastor and staff
probably feel alienated from or forgotten by denominational leaders and peers in churches whose communities
are not undergoing significant change. Relationships are
often strained; a communicated empathy is rare; peer
support is almost nonexistent.

This description could be enlarged upon in many
directions. In general terms it describes the situation in
several thousand churches in America today and
delineates the future of many other congregations.[4]

Addressing this kind of situation, churches have
operated under one of several options open to them
when they face these problems:

1. A congregation can choose to die a lingering, and
often painful, death. Many churches have made this
decision. Refusing to change, hostile to the new residents,
disappointed at those who no longer drive in from afar,
and always talking about the good old days when Dr. Great
Preacher was pastor, they lock themselves up behind
fortress walls and pass away.

2. A church can choose to die a sudden death. It can
sell or give its property away, urge its members to join
other churches, and officially vote to disband. This
provides immediate deliverance from the horns of the
dilemma, but it really solves few problems and usually is
done only after gaping wounds have been inflicted and
considerable agony of soul has been experienced. I
believe, however, it is to be preferred to the first option.

3. A church may choose to merge with another
congregation in the same community for any of several

reasons. If the merger is to combine resources to perpetuate the fortress mentality, this option is just an extension of option number one.

4. A church may choose to die with dignity. Some churches have decided to give the last years of their lives in meeting the physical and social needs of the peoples of the changing community. They commit their resources, facilities, and staff to this kind of ministry. The bulk of the membership is usually not directly involved. In the main, it is ministry by proxy. No real effort is made and no expectation is harbored that any of the people receiving these ministries will ever become a significant part of the membership of the church.

All four of these options could be reduced to one: a decision to die — for whatever reason and in whatever manner.

5. A fifth option is to relocate the meeting place of the church. There are two ways to go about this. The first is to merge with an already existing church in another community. A second is to buy property in another community and/or build a new building, begin to meet there, and attempt to develop a ministry in the new community.

This decision may be made at any one of several stages. The church may relocate early, when the influx of new people and the exodus of members from the community first begins. In this case, the building is usually sold and the resources used to erect a new building. At times a church will begin a satellite congregation in the community where it plans to relocate.

Second, the church may seek to develop another congregation or permit someone else to develop another congregation indigenous to the people moving into the community, using its own building as a meeting place. When the original church moves, it either sells or gives the building to the new congregation. Most strongly prefer to sell.

Third, if the community has become highly multi-ethnic or multi-racial, the church may opt before it departs to develop several congregations that meet

within its building. In fact, part of the original
congregation may stay to become one of the several
congregations that meets in the building.[5]

Fourth, a church may wait, maintaining a fortress
mentality until death is near, and then attempt to sell
and move. In this case it must sell; it no longer has the
vitality to begin from scratch again in a new community. Also, the residences of the members in such a
case are not usually grouped in any one place. Such a
move often ends in failure to continue the life and
ministry of the church. Attempting to save its life, it has
lost it.

As Lyle Schaller (1979), Ezra Earl Jones (1976), and
Gaylord Noyce (1975) have all intimated, there are good
reasons for relocation. Extraordinary care should be
taken to avoid laying a load of guilt on those churches and
church leaders who opt for this course of action.[6]

6. A church may decide to continue to meet in the
transitional community, to minister to and evangelize
the people in the community, to integrate the membership
with new members from the new residents of the
community, and eventually to become indigenous to the
community-as-it-has-become. This probably is
considered the most ideal and "Christian" option. It is
being advocated by many church and denominational
leaders, attempted by many churches, and carried on
successfully by a small but growing number. Even if this
is done successfully, it has some pitfalls; if unsuccessfully, it
has many.

7. A church may attempt type-transformation. For
example, a neighborhood church may deny it is a
neighborhood church and insist that it is a "metropolitan"
church with a ministry to the whole city. By "whole
city" it usually means those of the particular
socio-economic and racial group to which the bulk of
its commuters belong. This is another form of fortress
mentality. If the church is successful in drawing new
people from the larger city, it continues to ignore and be
isolated from the community in the immediate area of
its building. An "old First Church" may attempt to regain

its lost glory through adopting a "metropolitan" or "special purpose" church style. This is another way that this option is often exercised.

8. A congregation may choose to make a more deliberate, quicker, and cleaner transition to a church relevant to the community-as-it-has-become. C. Peter Wagner has outlined this approach, modeled after a plan to "indigenize" a national denominational body on an overseas mission field.[7] With this approach a date would be set two years in advance at which time a transition of leadership would be made from the people who commute to those who have been recruited from the new arrivals in the community. A co-pastor indigenous to the new people would be called, and intensive evangelistic efforts for the next two years would be made among the new residents. On a certain, predetermined date, the original pastor would resign, along with commuter church officers, and a total transition of leadership would be made.

Few churches have used this approach. It has many inherent problems. In churches with congregational government — and almost all American churches tend toward congregationalism — it would be next to impossible to achieve. It makes no provision for the protection and care of the original leadership, it seems to assume some higher authority which could order such action, and it would surely lead to many church divisions.

9. A church may choose to reproduce itself in the various cultures or subcultures of the community where it meets. I speak here of more than the various possibilities mentioned above for the church which opts to move. This option can be used in tandem with any of the options numbered four through seven. My thesis is that it should be used along with the other options.

For a church to opt to maintain only its meeting place in a community without aggressively addressing the gospel of Christ to the community and attempting to serve the people of the community in Jesus' name is most unfortunate and threatens the apostolic character of

the congregation as a church of Jesus Christ. It is an
option of needless, purposeless death. To merge in order
to take longer to die just prolongs the agony. In most
cases, to disband is not the best option either.

Whichever of the other options is chosen, the
congregation that meets in a changing community can
multiply its own witness and ministry among the new
residents by planting new congregations. Such a plan
should be part of a comprehensive strategy for that
changing or, better, "new" community. No strategy can be
comprehensive that does not include this option.

It is easy enough to see how this option can combine
with the option to move as described above. What is
more difficult to see is how this option can and should be
combined with the decision to die through ministry
(option four), the decision to make a speedy and forced
transition (option seven), or especially, the decision to
minister, evangelize, and eventually become indigenous
to the new people in the community. Surely, with this
last option, leaders tend to rationalize, the decision to
reproduce one's church in its own community through
daughter churches would be counterproductive.

Not at all. Let me repeat again, *it is impossible to
have a comprehensive strategy without planting new
congregations.* The strategies we have been using —
even the "best" and "most Christian" ones — have subtle
inadequacies. Very often they do not take seriously
enough the social realities created by the arrival of new
people and the flight of former residents.

WHAT WE HAVE BEEN DOING: A CRITIQUE

Let me suggest several areas, both practical and
conceptual, where our most advocated strategies can
be faulted. Anemic motivation and distorted viewpoint
have subtle ways of diluting highest ideals. Each of these
areas overlaps, and one leads, quite naturally, to another.

1. Most of the reasoned exhortation about the
church in the transitional community confuses the
building where the church meets with the body of

believers. The literature on the subject has repeated impassioned pleas for the church to "stay and serve," while in fact, the church has, in the main, already moved. That is just the problem. The church only meets for worship and to conduct social ministries in the community. The call to "stay and serve" is most often a call to *commute and serve.*

Ezra Earl Jones, who is usually very careful to speak precisely about all subjects, has a few sentences that illustrate the point. "But to remove a church from a community for the sole reason of maintaining it as an institution is unacceptable. . . . A church should never relocate from a community in transition when it is the only remaining church."[8] This is clear confusion of the church with the church house. To keep a church building open in a community only to maintain an institution is also unacceptable.

2. Related to the tendency to confuse the building with the church is an inconsistency concerning enlistment and support. Members of the old church in the transitional community are urged to continue to return to the community from which they have moved for worship and ministry. In fact, members are often accused of racism and escapism, of disloyalty and inadequate dedication if they consider uniting with a church in the community where they live. Their continued support in organizational roles, in various social ministries, and in monetary contributions, they are often told, is absolutely necessary if the congregation is to continue to survive and to minister.

At the same time, leaders do all they can to enlist new members from those newly arrived in the community. Most of the literature — most of our concern, I will suggest later — is for these older, prestigious churches, the flagships of our denominations, that are about to be lost. Little or no thought and no space in literature are given to those little congregations that meet in storefronts and remodeled warehouses, churches in which a large number of the new residents either hold membership or have given some level of support.

If our concern is for the *whole* Body of Christ (and not just for the "flagship" churches), shouldn't these new arrivals be urged to go back to their old communities in order to support their former storefront churches with bivocational pastors?

Most individuals responding to this question will insist that the varied and more holistic ministries offered by the larger, more stable churches and the more balanced leadership of a well trained, professional staff are adequate reasons for urging newcomers to identify with the well established congregations in their new community. The same arguments are used by leaders of growing suburban churches to attract those who have fled racially changing communities.

Isn't the basic problem that we can't bear to lose the great old institutions with their rich traditions and stately buildings?

3. Much of the literature about churches in transition reflects an inordinate concern for real estate. B. Carlisle Driggers is one of the most sensitive people I have ever met. He has demonstrated his compassion for and interest in persons as persons through years of leadership in churches attempting to minister in transitional communities. His book, *The Church in the Changing Community: Crisis or Opportunity,* is a passionate plea for Southern Baptists to "stay and minister" in changing communities. But he, too, falls into the real estate trap.

If we lose the great cities of our land, only chaos will be the result. . . . At some time in the future Southern Baptists may try to move back into the cities and relocate churches. When this occurs . . . it might be discovered that (1) property will be scarce and practically unavailable; (2) the properties which might be available will be anything but choice for church buildings or will have exorbitant price tags; and (3) the people living in the neighborhoods will not desire for Southern Baptist churches to be there at all because Southern Baptists departed them in the past when they were needed most.[9]

The major impact of this paragraph is "stay and hold on to the property!" The truth is that imposing, ornate, expensive buildings may appear so foreboding to the new arrivals that they effectively keep them from Christ and identification with his church.

One of the early studies of churches in transitional communities was made by Robert L. Wilson and James H. Davis in the mid-sixties. At the end of the book they considered the dilemma of denominational administrators who, among American Protestants at least, have little control over the action of local congregations. Conserving hard-won real estate was a major concern. The first question to be asked, according to Wilson and Davis, in an effort to discover guidelines for effective administrative procedures was, "What can be done to conserve the property assets of the churches located in communities which have completed their racial change?"[10] This concern is just below the surface in much of the literature discussing this issue. Its presence leaves one feeling that property is sometimes more important than people in our strategies for transitional churches.

4. Most of the published rhetoric and philosophy on transitional communities and churches is focused on the people who are leaving, not on those who are arriving. Communities are described according to the classical sociological categories. They move from the new development stage to the post-transitional stage.[11] The life cycle of institutions is applied to churches and collated with the stages of community development. The whole picture is one of decline and deterioration and decay, moving inevitably toward death.

This is all true from the point of view of the long-term residents. But from the perspective of the new residents, the community is one of hope, not despair. They are moving to better homes, leaving less desirable conditions. Jere Allen and George W. Bullard, Jr. have noted this condition in a well done booklet, *Hope for the Church in the Changing Community.*

The post-transitional stage . . . can be the newly developing stage of a community in disguise. The cycle of

*the community stages begins again, and new patterns
of relating . . . are established. . . . This is the real
opportunity for the church in the changing
community, i.e., the ability to perceive the new
community which is emerging and to build the future
band upon it.*[12]

Failure to see the social situation from the viewpoint of
the newcomer has tended to divert strategies toward
maintenance and survival goals. Evangelistic and servant
ministries addressed to newcomers are seen as a way to
perpetuate the institutions. The spiritual and moral reasons
for getting involved in these ministries are adulterated.

5. Consequently, much that has been done in local
churches has been motivated more by a concern for
sustaining the existing institutions than for meeting the
needs of people in the transitional community.
Institutional requirements—debt retirement, proper
maintenance of extensive buildings, staff to lead
sophisticated, middle-class programs, the support
necessary to guarantee open doors—easily intermingle
with Christlike concern for the unsaved and action
toward those who are hurting. Motivations become
mixed and unclear. The situation is often perceived early
by newcomers. They feel they are being used, and at
times they are.

The solution is not to abandon evangelistic and
servant ministries. The solution is to commit ourselves to
the most effective means for achieving goals related to
these ministries. Those who are already Christians need
to be enlisted and conserved. Those who are not
Christians need to find Christ. Individuals and groups in
transitional areas have open, aching wounds, spiritual
and physical, that need to be bound. For many of these
people the best way to help will *not* be to incorporate
them into the existing WASP congregations. Many will be
culturally uncomfortable in existing churches. If they
were to join, they would be involved in the support of
institutions (facilities, traditions, and goals) with which
they do not identify. They would be expected to express

their commitment to Christ in worship patterns largely alien to their culture. Other options need to be found.

6. Strategies used by old churches in transitional communities often express a cultural imperialism that is both offensive and oppressive to newcomers. We have tended to approach the whole matter of reaching new peoples from *our* perspective, for *our* needs, and with *our* methods. We have expected these new people, when they have become involved in our church, to adopt our worship patterns. Even though congregations make some concessions toward diversity in music, very few churches have moved to true pluralism in forms of worship.

Our strategy often reflects an assumption that the way in which the existing, established church worships is culturally acceptable to newcomers. We may assume that they will prefer it. Lurking in the back of our corporate ecclesiastical cranium is a firm conviction that when these newcomers are properly assimilated into our churches, they will appreciate the grand worship patterns we presently enjoy. Bach is, after all, better than the Blackwood Brothers. The gospel songs of the eighteenth century are superior to the gospel soul music of the twentieth century.

7. The strategies that we advocate, though we have the best of intentions, are often paternalistic at best and can be racist in their most extreme expressions. This is the most subtle of all the pitfalls I have mentioned.

The problem is not with what is done, but with the attitude that pervades it. Too often, the ministries in which we engage are only deeds we do for the "poor folks." Our evangelistic efforts are like much of the county jail evangelism in which I have often shared. No mutual repentance, no confession of sin is expressed on the part of the witnesses. Our message too often sounds like, "Be good like us," rather than, "Turn to Christ." Beneath ministries that we perform, there can be a subtle paternalism or prejudice based on race, class, national origin, or life style.

What we do may be altruistic. We may ourselves be

engaged in a terrible battle with overt racism. We may detest paternalism with a passion. We may give ourselves in selfless abandon to serving people. Yet our basic attitude and approach are demeaning to those who receive our ministry. The end result is that the newcomers are not built up but belittled. There is no affirmation of their culture, no appreciation of their roots. Thus, much that we do, even though it actually brings substantial help to those who receive it, turns them away from Jesus Christ rather than attracting them to him.

TOWARD A MORE COMPREHENSIVE AND EFFECTIVE STRATEGY

Alerted to some of the pitfalls that plague the various solutions which have been fashioned for churches in transitional communities, we can move on to explore church planting as a manageable and viable option in these rapidly changing urban areas.

Everyone concerned with this problem agrees that a more effective and extensive strategy is needed. Such a strategy should also be theologically and culturally aware. It should avoid as far as possible the subtle weaknesses of existing strategy models. Action plans we have developed for urban transitional areas have too often been ineffective and have never been comprehensive.

A bold determination to begin new congregations among some of the new residents, I assert, is part of the answer. A church planting plan will enable a church to design a more holistic strategy. This more comprehensive strategy should be aimed at the penetration of every significant social segment within the church's community, a community which has probably become increasingly pluralistic.

First, let me identify a basic assumption upon which this discussion is based. I assume that the churches we are discussing have abandoned any serious commitment to racial exclusivism in their membership.

This has been made clear in earlier chapters of this book. Nevertheless, it must be restated here. The

concepts I advocate must not be construed as defenses
for racially or socially segregated churches. Every church
should win to Christ and incorporate into its
membership as many as it can from the various racial,
social, and language-culture groups within the
community where it meets for worship. I agree with
Donald A. McGavran, who wrote:

*Nothing I have said justifies injustice and intolerance,
or the strong enforcing segregation against the weak. My
own considered opinion is that, in the United States,
the refusal of any congregation to admit Negroes as
members is sin.*[13]

A church that is not willing to evangelize, baptize, and
welcome into its membership those of other races and
classes is as heretical as those that deny that Jesus
Christ died for our sins and was raised for our justification.

The question with which we struggle is not how to
inculcate the principles of Christian brotherhood in a
congregation. That is a serious problem within many
congregations and should be addressed. But that is not the
problem we address here. If a church is racially
segregated in a racially changing community, it must
either flee or die. I assume in this discussion that the
churches have already passed that Rubicon and are
committed to evangelizing and ministering effectively to
all peoples.

The question we address is not, "How should
Christians act toward peoples of different races and
cultures?" but "How can a church in a transitional
community effectively communicate Christ to all the
various cultures and subcultures of that community?"

I assume that the problem is not with the policy of the
church. The problem is with the socio-cultural attitudes
and feelings *of the new residents of the community.* A
church may be eager to receive anyone into its
fellowship who gives evidence of knowing Christ and
wants to follow him in daily life, and still find it
impossible to disciple the new arrivals effectively.

In response to this problem I make three suggestions that will move toward a more comprehensive and effective strategy in transitional communities.

1. *Develop a people-vision.* In America we tend to idealize the individual and perceive society as essentially composed of isolated or, at best, loosely related individuals. The programs most often suggested for churches in transitional communities reflect this basic viewpoint. They are designed for and directed toward individuals without serious reference to the social structures found in the transitional community. There are numerous reasons why this is true.

Most often Americans are taught that differences are bad; *that we should refuse to be* stereotyped; *that each of us is a unique individual, and* not *merely a member of a group.*[14]

We have been nurtured on two myths. The first is that America is a melting pot where different ethnic and social groups lose their distinctiveness. The second is that the cultural distinctives are to be lost in "Anglo conformity."[15] In spite of gargantuan efforts to make it so, America is not a melting pot, but as Andrew M. Greeley has suggested, a stewpot.[16] Components remain distinct.

Ethnic pluralism in America is an accepted reality in most academic disciplines and in the political, educational, and business communities of the nation. In denominational and local church planning, ethnic realities have been but slowly recognized. The new ethnic consciousness that arose out of the civil rights movement of the sixties makes many of us uneasy. We have difficulty recognizing the various people-groups created by racial, cultural, and social distinctives. When we do perceive these groups we often do not appreciate and adequately value those things that define their peoplehood.[17]

In a changing urban community, the first step toward developing a comprehensive strategy is to take these distinctions seriously. We must develop a sensitivity to peoples rather than just to individuals. We must begin to ask ourselves how we can reach a whole people rather than individuals.

2. *Recognize the diversity within people groups.* While it is crucial to develop an eye for discerning groups of people within a community, it is equally important that we recognize the heterogeneity within these larger homogeneous groups.[18] Church leaders tend to think that any people-group different from their own is a cultural monolith. That is, of course, a type of people-blindness. Strategies developed that do not give serious consideration to in-group diversity will be ineffective.

Each people-group moving into a transitional community can be described and graphed in terms of its predictable responsiveness to the church already meeting in that community. By defining the level of ethnic consciousness among the newcomers, an acceptable estimate of responsiveness to a different group can be obtained.

Daniel R. Sanchez, in his seminal effort to develop a five-year growth plan for the Baptist Convention of New York, formulated the following hypothesis: "The assimilation status of a group determines the degree of cultural awareness that will be present in the church established by the group."[19] Adapting from Andrew M. Greeley, he categorized ethnic groups as:

(1) *Nuclear Ethnics: those explicitly and self-consciously concerned about ethnic tradition;*

(2) *Fellow Traveler Ethnics: those to whom ethnicity is a relatively important part of self-conscious identification;*

(3) *Marginal Ethnics: those who occasionally think of themselves as ethnics; and*

(4) *Assimilated Ethnics: those who explicitly and self-consciously exclude themselves from ethnic collectivity.*[20]

These general categories are descriptive of the various subcultures among any significant people-group moving to a community in transition. With them in mind, I wish to formulate a corollary to Sanchez's hypothesis: *The degree of assimilation among a new people-group will determine its openness to integration with existing churches in urban transitional communities.*

What does this mean? First, churches in transitional communities can realistically expect only a certain portion of a new people-group to identify with the existing WASP church. They can expect to evangelize effectively that portion of the people-group that is "assimilated." With some adjustments in style and leadership, they may expect to reach a portion of those classified as "marginal." The second thing it means is that a game plan is needed for the remainder of the people-group that will include efforts in addition to those designed to attach people to the existing churches.

The predictable responsiveness can be depicted by use of a Gaussian graph. Karl Friedrich Gauss, a German mathematician, discovered the most human character-istics, when plotted against populations, produce a curve which looks like a gently sloping round-topped mountain.[21]

The four degrees of assimilation discussed above will be distributed in different proportions for different people-groups. The size of each sub-group will be determined by certain related factors: racial identifica-tion, national origin, religion, economic status, vocation, formal schooling, regional identification, length of time in America, etc.[22] Figure 1 shows how the four categories might be distributed among a typical American black people-group. Figure 2 represents the distribution among a Hispanic group. Figure 3 pictures a people-group of Indo-Chinese refugees.

3. *Adopt a balanced strategy designed to communi-cate Christ to all the peoples of the transitional community.*

FIGURE 1. **Assimilation Factors among Blacks**

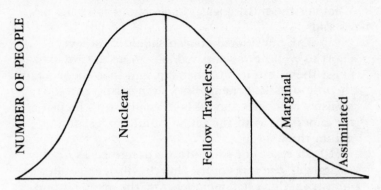

FIGURE 2. **Assimilation Factors among Hispanics**

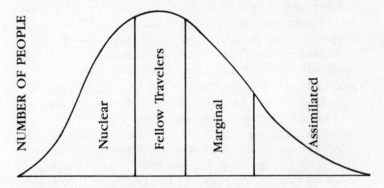

FIGURE 3. **Assimilation Factors among Laotians**

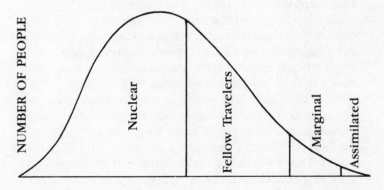

What are the missiological implications for what has been said?[23]

(a) The transitional church should make every effort to win the "assimilated" subgroup to Christ, to enlist them into its membership, and then incorporate them into its leadership. Both evangelistic and ministry strategies should be formulated to focus on these persons with the intent of full integration within the church.

(b) To reach for Christ those described as "marginal," the transitional church will need to alter its ministry style. A staff member from the people-group and an effort to include some worship forms from the culture of the newcomers may suffice if the number in this subgroup is relatively small. If a significant number of the people-group are at this level of assimilation or if there are multiple people-groups within the community, the transitional church may need to become a multiculture church or organize a new multiculture congregation. An alternative may be to constitute several mono-culture churches that will share its building.

(c) Those newcomers who are classified as "fellow travelers" require a bilingual or bi-cultural church to respond most easily to the claims of Christ. In this kind of church "fellow travelers" can express their Christianity most naturally and exercise their leadership most comfortably. This subgroup will probably eventually require a new congregation. If the newcomers are part of a language-culture group, the way to begin may be with a separate department. If they are from an English-speaking racial group, "fellow travelers" will probably require their own congregation from the beginning. Starting new congregations may prove to be the most effective method of bringing this group as a whole to Christ.

(d) Those who are unassimilated, the "nuclear" type, require a church indigenous in language, culture, and, as far as possible, leadership. A new congregation is an absolute necessity for the most effective evangelism with this group. They demand a church that looks, sounds, and functions as part of their culture. Church planting is the only faithful response to the missionary command of Jesus among these people.

The complex social structure of transitional communities demands a complex missionary strategy. A strategy is needed that will consider the social diversity within the community in all of its aspects. To penetrate each people-group with Christ's good news and to gather those who believe into responsible churches should be the primary goal of the strategy. To maintain the existing institution should not be the first consideration. The diversity within people-groups will permit both effective evangelism and a continued vigorous life for existing churches. A complex strategy makes it possible for a church to respond realistically to the community-as-it-is-becoming.

George W. Bullard, Jr., in a dissertation that should be required reading for those who wrestle with the problems of churches in transitional communities, studied 100 selected Southern Baptist churches in metropolitan transitional communities in 1975. These 100 churches had been studied in 1965 by G. Willis Bennett.[24] Bullard set out to update the social research on the churches after ten years, to discover trends and make suggestions for future ministry.[25] One of his conclusions was that "churches with a perceived ministry style of evangelism tend not to decline statistically."[26]

Bullard found that the way a church perceived itself and its various ministries was of more importance than what the church did. Churches that did not decline statistically were, along with many that did decline, involved in intensive community ministries. The nondeclining churches perceived various community ministries as means to obey Christ's evangelistic mandate. These churches served in order to win to faith in Christ. They understood themselves to be meeting needs in the name of Christ in order to be able to legitimately call people to faith in Christ. Commitment to a comprehensive evangelistic strategy will tend toward both missionary obedience and institutional longevity.

The rechurching of American inner cities is under way. Most of it has been spontaneous, unplanned, and unowned by the most prominent conciliar and evangelical denominations. No comprehensive program design for churches in the transitional communities has included intentional church planting as one of its action plans. Church planting is an untried, overlooked option for the urban transitional community. The day for its consideration has come.

Urban transitional communities need to be considered mission fields in the same way that other under-churched areas of America are considered mission fields.[27] But the responsibility for congregationalizing the new people-groups in urban transitional areas should rest first of all on the existing churches, not on the regional or national judiciaries and agencies of denominations.

Both interdenominational and intradenominational cooperation are still necessary, however, in addressing the transitional communities of our nation. Existing churches should adopt a comprehensive and pluralistic strategy as early as possible in the process of change. Church planting enables churches in transitional communities to have a balanced and effective approach to the total community.

NOTES

[1]Ezra Earl Jones, "Identifying the Church in the Racially Changing Community," in *Churches in Racially Changing Communities,* Proceedings of the National Leadership Conference, Department of Cooperative Ministries with National Baptists, Home Mission Board, Southern Baptist Convention, 1978, p. 33, defines churches in transitional communities as "congregations located in geographical areas . . . where change is occurring that is basic to the character of the community; where change is widespread, and where the fundamental nature of the community . . . will be radically different for at least a generation."

[2]PRRC *Emerging Trends,* Vol. 2, No. 1, p. 2.

[3]For example, Ezra Earl Jones, "Rationale Question, and Assumptions," in *New Church Development in the Eighties,* Ezra Earl Jones, ed. (New York: National Division, Board of Global Ministries, the United Methodist Church, 1976), pp. 8, 9, seems to promise a great deal but in his later book, *Strategies for New Churches* (New York: Harper & Row, Publishers, 1976), pp. 168-170, gives very little attention to the possibility. Lyle E. Schaller raised this possibility in his early book *Planning for Protestantism in Urban America* (Nashville: Abingdon Press, 1965), pp. 154-156, but concluded that the need in declining communities was for more professional staff not more churches. C. Peter Wagner in *Your Church Can Be Healthy* (Nashville: Abingdon Press, 1979) does not mention this as a major option for a church with "ethnikitus," but a church planting model is described in his *Our Kind of People* (Atlanta: John Knox Press, 1979), pp. 158-163.

[4]For more adequate descriptions of the problems that arise in transitional communities see Schaller, *Planning for Protestantism,* pp. 157-161; Robert Lee, ed., *Cities and Churches: Reading on the Urban Church* (Philadelphia: The Westminster Press, 1962), pp. 85-124; Review and Expositor, LXIII (Summer, 1966), a whole issue given to "The Church in the Changing Community"; G. Willis Bennett, *Confronting a Crisis* (Atlanta: Home Mission Board, SBC, 1967), pp. 1-13; George A. Torney, ed., *Toward Creative Urban Strategy* (Waco, TX: Word Books, Publisher, 1970), pp. 5-23; Lyle E. Schaller, *Hey, That's Our Church* (Nashville: Abingdon Press, 1975), pp. 39 ff.; Gaylord B. Noyce, *Survival and Mission for the City Church* (Philadelphia: The Westminster Press, 1975), p. 68 ff.; Walter E. Ziegenhals, *Urban Churches in Transition* (New York: The Pilgrim Press, 1978), p. 13 ff.; Ezra Earl Jones and Robert L. Wilson, *What's Ahead for Old First Church* (New York: Harper and Row, Publishers, 1974), pp. 9-50; Robert L. Wilson and James H. Davis, *The Church in the Racially Changing Community* (Nashville: Abingdon Press, 1966), p. 19 ff.; Murray H. Leiffer, *The Effective City Church* (Nashville: Abingdon-Cokesbury Press, 1946) p. 82 ff.; Ezra Earl Jones, art. cit. and "The Church that Wants to Remain in the Changing Community," *Churches in Racially Changing Communities,* 1978, pp. 57-89; B. Carlisle Driggers, *The Church in the Changing Community: Crisis or Opportunity* (Atlanta: Home Mission Board, SBC, 1977), pp. 14-21; George W. Bullard, Jr., "An Analysis of Change in Selected Southern Baptist Churches in Metropolitan Transitional Communities," unpublished Th.M. dissertation, Southern Baptist Theological Seminary, Louisville, Kentucky, 1976, p. 14 ff.; B. Carlisle Driggers, *Models of Metropolitan Ministry* (Nashville: Broadman Press, 1979); Francis M. DuBose, *How Churches Grow in an Urban World* (Nashville: Broadman Press, 1978), p. 145 ff.; G. Peter Wagner, *Your Church Can Be Healthy,* p. 29 ff.; Douglas Alan Walrath, *Leading Churches Through Change* (Nashville: Abingdon Press, 1979); and

Jere Allen and George W. Bullard, Jr., *Hope for the Church in the Changing Community,* (mimeographed book; Atlanta: Home Mission Board, SBC: 1980), pp. 11-30.

[5]Daniel R. Sanchez, "A Five Year Plan of Growth for the Ministry of the Baptist Convention of New York in the Area of Evangelism," unpublished doctoral dissertation, Fuller Theological Seminary, 1979, has a very excellent discussion of this option.

[6]Jones, *Strategies,* pp. 158-161; Lyle E. Schaller, *Effective Church Planning* (Nashville: Abingdon, 1979), pp. 143-145; and Noyce, *Survival and Mission,* pp. 76-79. Note the last two especially for the guilt factor.

[7]Wagner, *Your Church Can Be Healthy,* pp. 37-39.

[8]Jones, *Strategies,* p. 159.

[9]Driggers, *Crisis or Opportunity,* pp. 12, 13.

[10]Wilson and Davis, *Church in Racially Changing Community,* p. 143.

[11]See Jones, "Identifying the Church in the Racially Changing Community," pp. 38-45, and Jones and James D. Anderson, *The Management of Ministry* (New York: Harper and Row, Publishers, 1978), pp. 38-41; Larry McSwain, "Stages of Community Transition," *Proceedings of National Leadership Conference* on Churches in Racially Changing Communities (mimeographed; Atlanta: Home Mission Board, SBC, 1979), pp. 104-116; and Allen and Bullard, *Hope,* pp. 13-26.

[12]Allen and Bullard, *Hope,* p. 20. See also Jones, "Identifying the Church," pp. 45, 46.

[13]Donald A. McGavran, *Understanding Church Growth* (Grand Rapids: William B. Eerdmans Publishing Company, 1970), p. 209.

[14]Michael Novak, "Preface to the Paperback Edition," *The Rise of the Unmeltable Ethnics* (Macmillan Paperback Edition; New York: Macmillan Publishing Co., Inc., 1975), p. XVI.

[15]Peter Wagner, *Our Kind of People,* discusses this fully, pp. 34-57.

[16]Andrew M. Greeley, "Catholics Prosper while the Church Crumbles," *Psychology Today,* June 1976, p. 44.

[17]The definition of a "people" adopted by the Lausanne Committee is the background of the following discussion. A people is "a significantly large sociological grouping of individuals who perceive themselves to have a common affinity for one another." Edward R. Dayton, *That Everyone May Hear* (Monrovia, CA: MARC, 1979), p. 22.

[18]The most detailed study of this social reality from a church growth point of view is Wagner, *Our Kind of People,* pp. 58-77.

[19]Sanchez, "A Five Year Plan," p. 244.

[20]*Ibid.,* 243, 244. See Andrew M. Greeley, "Is Ethnicity Unamerican?" *New Catholic World,* pp. 106-109.

[21]See Wilfred Brown, *Organization* (London: Heinemann Education Books, Ltd., 1971), pp. 50, 51.

[22]Wagner, *Our Kind of People,* pp. 61-74, describes these different factors as contributors to one's "Ethclass."

[23]I am indebted to Daniel Sanchez for the following discussion. Sanchez, "Five Year Plan," pp. 244-246.
[24]See Bennett, *Confronting a Crisis.*
[25]Bullard, "An Analysis of Change," pp. 1, 2.
[26]*Ibid.,* p. 104. See also George W. Bullard, Jr., "What Is Happening with Churches in Metropolitan Transitional Areas?" *Search,* Summer 1979, pp. 32-39.
[27]Bullard, "An Analysis of Change," p. 106.

Appendix

Congregationalizing and Evangelizing in Today's City

*A Paper Given at the
National Consultation
on Urban Evangelism,
St. Louis
November 20-22, 1980
Sponsored by the
Evangelism Section of the
Home Mission Board,
Southern Baptist Convention*

In order to speak
intelligently
about evangelism
in the cities,
we must acknowledge
two important facts.
The first fact is
that there are
significant numbers
of ethnic,
or culturally distinct,
persons in the
metropolitan areas
of our country.
We cannot
realistically
talk about winning
our cities for Christ
unless we make plans
to reach these
ethnic persons
with the gospel.
The second fact is
that a special type
of evangelism
is needed to reach
ethnic persons
for Christ.
The message must be
transculturated
if it is to be
meaningful
to the recipient group.

Daniel R. Sanchez, 1980

Since America already has over 335,000
churches and over 10 percent of the total are affiliated with
the Southern Baptist Convention,[1] and since any
windshield survey will reveal that numerous churches
can be found in all parts of the cities of America, the
questions I must answer are:

1. *Do we need new churches in our cities?*
2. *Is church planting essentially related to the task of
   effective evangelism in our cities?*
3. *If so, what does such a need require of us?*

I

Does America really need new churches? Isn't it, after
all, the better part of wisdom to stimulate the spiritual
vitality of existing churches and to produce more
evangelistic effectiveness in these congregations?
Towering steeples and tumbledown storefront
churches can be seen on every street in our cities. What
kind of evidence could possibly suggest that more
churches are needed?

    1. *Great unchurched populations in America,
especially in the metropolitan centers, demand new*

churches. The new census will show that we have about
225 million people in this nation. You may not have
noticed, but they are not all active in a local church, nor
do they all behave like disciples of Jesus Christ.

For the purposes of our discussion, this huge
population can be divided into three large groups.[2]
Group one we will call the *Insiders*. They are true
disciples. They are sincere, ardent believers in Jesus Christ.
They follow him in their private and public lives. They
are active in the churches. They number about 55
million.[3]

Group two we will call the *Sometimers*. They are only
nominal Christians, marginal disciples. They are
"believers," but this fact never seriously affects the way
they think or act. They number about 90 million.

Group three we will call *Outsiders*. They make no claims
to be disciples of Christ. They are, rather, followers of
the great religions and cults of the East; they are Muslims
and Marxists; they are hedonists and humanists; they
are secularists and animists; they are agnostics and
members of the Amalgamated Flying Saucers Clubs of
America; they are members of assertiveness training
seminars and Full Moon Meditation Groups.

Let's focus on the Outsiders first. They belong to no
church and do not consider themselves Christians. They
are fellow Democrats or fellow Republicans. They live on
our streets. We meet them in the supermarket and in
the shopping mall. They attend school functions. Many of
them teach in our public school systems. They work in
our banks. They own our service stations. They belong to
our labor unions and tennis clubs and attend the
municipal opera in our city. "Most of them are very nice
people, but they wouldn't be offended if someone
described them as pagans."[4]

Outsiders have either quietly rejected Christ or have
never been inclined to take his claims seriously. Some hear
the Christian message with a strong, traditional bias.
Many Outsiders believe that man and history are mindless
accidents that happen because of the right mixture of
materials in a warm and wet environment. Many Outsiders

are total secularists and materialists. Others are devoted humanists. Still others are "true believers," entirely devoted to religious systems different from the Christian faith. Other Outsiders are hedonists, committed only to personal pleasure. Most are hard workers, enthusiastic, devoted to education, career, and the good life.

The Outsiders in America number around 80 million. Only six other nations in the world — Russia, Japan, China, India, Indonesia and Brazil — have a total population that exceeds 80 million. America is one of the great mission fields of the world!

That is not, of course, the whole picture. We need to consider very carefully the Sometimers as well. Baptists, of all Christians, should be most dissatisfied with ignoring marginal disciples. We espouse the concept of the gathered church, the conviction that only deliberate disciples of Jesus should hold membership in the visible church. Yet we are told that almost two out of five Southern Baptists are now nonresident church members. We also are painfully aware, though few people have counted them, that at least one out of five, though he is resident, is uninvolved and may well be living a scandalous life as far as the church is concerned.

What is true of Southern Baptists is generally true for other denominations in America also. When one adds the Sometimers and the Outsiders together one has about 170 million people who are not following Jesus Christ.

These figures are in no way precise. They have not been corrected for the percentage of the population under twelve years of age. It is difficult to decide exactly who is an Outsider and who is a Sometimer. Christians have very different standards by which they judge who should be called an Insider. Nevertheless, whatever standards are used, the overwhelming fact is that millions of Americans are unevangelized and unchurched.

Two other facts complicate the matter. One is that a large percentage of the Outsiders identify themselves as Ethnics. They cannot effectively be reached for Christ by existing evangelical churches. If they are won, it will be in churches where they feel comfortable and hear the Good News in the language of their hearts. We will discuss this point further a little later.

The second complication is the fact that the vast majority of the Outsiders and Sometimers are living in the great cities of our land. These are the very places where we have the fewest number of churches, proportionately. For example, 35.4 percent of the American population lives in the twenty-five largest Standard Metropolitan Statistical Areas (SMSA) of the nation. In 1978, only 12.4 percent of Southern Baptist resident members lived in those twenty-five SMSA's. Only 8.7 percent of their existing churches were located in those SMSA's. When one considers the total 272 SMSA's in the nation, the picture is not greatly improved. All SMSA's contain 73.3 percent of the total U.S. population. Southern Baptists have 51.9 percent of their members and 38.2 percent of their churches in these areas.[5] This means that 62 percent of the Southern Baptist churches are responsible for evangelizing 27 percent of the total population.

When we focus on the twenty-five largest SMSA's alone, 91 percent of our churches are attempting to evangelize 64 percent of the total U.S. population. Less than 9 percent of the churches are responsible for evangelizing 36 percent of the population. The great unchurched populations of America, mostly located in these metropolitan areas, demand new churches.

2. *Moral conditions in the country loudly shout for many more churches.* In June 1979, George Gallup, Jr., reporting on the statistical studies he had made attempting to assess the shape of the eighties, made the following comments:

"Violence, crime, and lawlessness pervade our society. In our annual studies conducted by the Charles F. Kettering Foundation, discipline is named by parents in communities of all sizes as the top problem facing the schools in their communities.

Street crime in the nation has reached frightening

proportions – one out of four of us has been mugged,
robbed, assaulted, or had his or her home broken into
at least once in a twelve-month period. But we are also,
in the minds of most Americans, suffering from
"white-collar" crime and immorality.

Furthermore, hundreds of teachers are physically
attacked each month by their students, and thousands of
school children are physically abused. A recent Gallup
Youth Survey indicated that as many as one teenager in
five is fearful of bodily injury during school hours.

Alcohol abuse and drug dependency among youth are
reaching epidemic proportions, reflecting a growing
trend in society as a whole. We continue to have a
serious drug problem on the college campuses of
America as indicated by the Gallup College Survey.

All signs point to the fact that the United States is
suffering a moral crisis of the first dimension."[6]

I conclude from this that we desperately need more
outposts of righteousness planted among every segment
of American society.

3. *Large numbers of homogeneous people-groups,*
who define their existence in terms of ethnic, racial, or
cultural values, or in terms of socio-economic
conditions or life styles prove that America needs
thousands of new churches.

Three sociological facts confront us. First, these
people-groups are here. Evangelical and conciliar
Protestants have been very slow to recognize the reality
of cultural diversity. Southern Baptists have, far beyond
any other Protestant group, responded to the social and
cultural variety that is America. However, leaders in
evangelism, even within the Home Mission Board, have
resisted the importance of ethnicity. Some have insisted
that all we need is a warm church, a clear message, and a
passion for the soul of the ethnic. That view, in my
opinion, stems from an irresponsible evangelism and an
inadequate theology. While the theology of ethnicity is
beyond the purview of this paper, I will say that it is God
who has formed and is forming the clans and tribes of

man, and it is his purpose that the beauty and character of
Jesus be formed among every people-group of the
world. That purpose includes all those groups who make
up the United States of America.

America is a nation of immigrants, and it can only be
properly perceived when one views its composition as
consisting of many peoples. America, as it is often said now,
was never a "melting pot." It is rather "a stewpot" where
each distinct cultural ingredient contributes to the
overall national flavor but retains its own distinctives.[7]
The mix is not just in black and white. It is a magnificent
tapestry, a multi-cultural, multi-colored masterpiece of
humanity.

Ethnics in America communicate in 157 distinct
languages.[8] They marry primarily within their own cultural
groups. They guard their languages, cherish national
costumes and customs, and celebrate the traditional
festivals of their people.

The number of such people-groups is increasing, and the
number of people within most groups is multiplying
rapidly. The proportion of persons who identify
themselves as ethnics increased significantly between
1970 and 1980. This proportion will continue to enlarge
during the rest of this century. Prior to 1978,
government agencies were saying that about 4 million
legal immigrants would be admitted each decade. But
immigration quotas have been exploded by the influx of
refugees during the last three years. *Newsweek* reported
recently that 1 million new people each year are settling
into the United States, both legally and illegally, and that
the change in landscape is obvious even to the untrained
eye.[9]

Who are these people-groups? There are 23 million
Latinos in many diverse sub-groups, 4 million Italians,
6 million Germans, 2.5 million Poles, 2 million Russians,
3 million Arabs, 3 million Asians more diverse from each
other than the various European peoples, and many other
smaller groups. In addition to newer arrivals, there are
23 million blacks and 1.2 million American Indians in
almost 500 tribes and clans. All together, these total

around 60 million, about 25 percent of the total
population.

A second sociological fact is that most of the evangelical
churches in America are English-speaking and, whether
white or black, are middle-class or have middle-class
aspirations. These congregations can, indeed, win some
of these millions and incorporate them into their
fellowships. But the most effective way to evangelize
most of the unchurched among these groups is through
churches where the Good News is proclaimed and
leadership is expressed by peers and where the Good
News can be celebrated in cultural forms dear to the
hearts of the people.

The third sociological fact is that the majority of
these people are in our great cities. Let me give a few
examples. According to *La Luz,* 64 percent of Hispanics
lived in thirty SMSA's in 1976.[10] In 1976, census
authorities estimated that 83.9 percent of Hispanic-
Americans were living in metropolitan areas. Twelve
metropolitan areas contained 3,700,000 Italian-Americans.
In 1970, almost 50 percent of the American Indians in the
U.S. lived in metropolitan areas. Almost 70 percent of the
Vietnamese refugees that have been settled are now
living in six major metropolitan areas. These merely
illustrate a fact that is already known.

What is my conclusion? Hundreds of ethnic, racial,
and socio-economic people-groups make up the
population of America. The number reaches into the
thousands when one considers the subtle but real
sub-culture distinctions within each significant
people-group. These groups are clustered in our cities.
God looks on these groups and our cities and says to us
as he said to Paul concerning the Corinthians, "Do not be
afraid . . . but go on speaking and do not be silent for I
am with you . . . for I have many people in this city" (Acts
18:9, 10). Thousands of these men and women can be
reconciled to God and become members of the Body of
Christ. If they are reached in significant numbers, it will
be through ethnic churches designed to incorporate them
with their ethnic brothers and sisters. The presence of

this variety of ethnic and racial groups provides abundant reasons for us to plant thousands of new churches in our cities. The multitude of unevangelized and unchurched persons in all walks of life and the moral crisis that has left the nation halted and maimed in character and vision provide further overwhelming evidence that we need new churches.

II

Is church planting essentially related to the task of effective evangelism in our cities? Is church planting actually a significant part of the church's mission at the end of the twentieth century?

My answer is a resounding, "Yes!" I believe that church planting is preeminently an apostolic task of the church. But church planting is crucial not only because of its biblical basis but also because of its evangelistic effectiveness.

Let's turn to the biblical basis first. Jesus said, "All authority has been given to Me in heaven and on earth. Wherever you go, make disciples of all the ethnic groups of man [*ta ethne* refers to the families, clans, and tribes of man, not to modern nations, whose boundaries usually include many *ta ethne*], baptizing them in the name of the Father and the Son and the Holy Spirit, teaching them to observe all that I commanded you; and lo, I am with you all the days, even to the end of the age."

We must ask ourselves how the early church moved out in obedience to this command. The answer is, "By congregationalizing and evangelizing." We must be careful that we always keep those two together. And I believe the order I have given them is important. These men planted house-churches all over the Mediterranean world, primarily in the cities, and from those bases of operation, the various culture groups were evangelized outward to the perimeters.

The apostolic office is directly related to church planting. In my opinion, many men and women in the contemporary church possess the apostolic gift.

Many of us are threatened by the words you have just read. But I am convinced that we have been blinded by our language habits and have not really taken time to see what the Bible says about the apostolic gift. We have failed to distinguish between the *Twelve* and the *apostles*. Only five times in the gospels are the Twelve referred to as the *twelve apostles* or the *twelve disciples*. Only five times in the gospels are the Twelve referred to with the word *apostle* alone. But twenty-five times in the gospels these twelve handpicked disciples of Jesus are called "the Twelve." We have confused the particular office of the *Twelve* with the office of *apostle* in the early church. The Twelve *were* apostles, but there are at least twelve other persons who are called apostles in the New Testament. The word *apostle* means "sent one," and the Twelve (the Eleven and Mathaias) were all "sent ones," but Barnabas and Silas and Paul and Andronicus and Janius—and men we've never heard of—were also numbered among the apostles.

There were only twelve in the special group of eyewitnesses to the ministry, death, and resurrection of Jesus—only twelve. That group has not been continued. We have their witness recorded in the New Testament. But there are many apostles and, in 1 Corinthians 12 and Ephesians 4, the gift of being an *apostle* is listed as one of the gifts of the risen Christ to his Church.

What was an apostle to do? Let's look at Paul. We have more information about him than we have about other apostles. We speak of Paul as a great evangelist, and he certainly had a gift for evangelism. Every apostle must have. But Paul never once called himself an evangelist. We preach sermons using Paul as a model pastor-teacher, and he certainly exercised pastoral and teaching gifts. He has become the great teacher of the Church. But never once did he call himself a pastor-teacher. Inspired of the Holy Spirit, Paul listed the character-requirements necessary for one who would be a bishop or pastor, but he never claimed that office for himself, even one time. However, he called himself an apostle twenty times.

If the word *apostle* is not restricted to the smaller number of special witnesses of Jesus, what is an *apostle?* Paul explained in 1 Corinthians 3. He was attempting to correct a church that had fallen into disunity and party spirit. He said: "What then is Apollos? And what is Paul? Servants through whom you believed, even as the Lord gave . . . to each one. I planted, Apollos watered, but God was causing the growth. . . . According to the grace of God which was given to me, as a master builder I laid a foundation and another is building upon it" (1 Cor. 3:5-10).

The role of an apostle is the role of a planter. Paul goes on to say in 1 Corinthians 9 that the seal, the proof of his apostleship was the church that he gathered in Corinth (1 Cor. 9:2). The proof of apostleship is the gathered, the planted church. Just as the proof of the prophet is the truth of his message and the proof of the evangelist is the fruit of his ministry, the seal of the apostle is the church he has called together.

In our day, with many established churches, the role of the pastor-teacher and the evangelist have been magnified. That has been needed. But the time has come for us to recognize the significance of the apostolic role in modern America. That role is one that lays foundations, that gathers congregations, that plants churches among new or at least different people-groups. These then become the foundation from which effective evangelism can be done in the city, as each congregation shares the Good News from household to household among all its web of relationships in its community. Someone will object: "We already have the churches. The foundations are already laid." Yes, thank God, we now have many churches. But I have already shown that we do not have enough for the multitudes of unchurched people in America. I will go further and say that the churches we have are primarily planted among two large, prominent people-groups in the city: middle-class, English-speaking whites and lower middle-class English-speaking blacks that are moving toward middle-class. It is un-Christian to insist that the only way "poor" white folks or upper middle-class white folks living in the city can become Christians is within a black afro-culture church. It is un-Christian to insist that if a Chicano or a black university professor wants to become a Christian, he must do it in a red-neck, white, English-speaking church in the city. What Paul and Barnabas resisted vigorously at the Jerusalem Conference (Acts 15) was a movement toward insisting that if a Gentile wanted to become a Christian, he had to do it within a Jewish-culture church.

First century apostles planted churches in all the cities around the Mediterranean Sea. Those churches do not exist today. That area is now *most* unresponsive to the gospel. There *are* churches existing there that are direct descendents of those planted by the early apostles. But these churches refused to congregationalize or evangelize the new people-groups that moved in over the centuries. At the meeting of the World Council of Churches' Commission on World Mission and Evangelism in Melbourne, Australia, two years ago (May, 1980), when confronted with a document on Christian witness, the Armenian archbishop of Jerusalem exclaimed, "But this means I must go out into the streets of Jerusalem, call Jews and Muslims together and preach to them. I have no intention of doing this . . . was the WCC formed to make more churches?"[11]

I do not know why the WCC was formed. I do know that if we stop planting new churches among the unchurched people of our cities and nation, we are moving toward the same kind of mentality.

We need more churches today for the same reason that churches needed to be multiplied in Paul's day: to become outposts of evangelistic extension among the various peoples of our cities. Effective evangelizing waits on adequate congregationalizing today just as in the first century.

Looking at the biblical material is only one way of demonstrating that church planting is essentially related to evangelism. Research reveals that smaller and newer churches are more effective in terms of evangelism than larger and older churches.

This is true, in general, among all Protestant groups. Lyle E. Schaller said recently:

"The most important single argument for making new church development a high priority is this is the most effective means for reaching unchurched persons. Numerous studies have shown that 60 to 80 percent of the new adult members of new congregations are persons who were not actively involved in the life of any worshipping congregation immediately prior to joining that new mission. By contrast, most long established churches draw the majority of their new adult members from persons who transfer in from other congregations. New Christians as well as young adults born since 1940 are found in disproportionately larger numbers in new missions than in the older churches."[12]

What is true in general for all American Protestants is also true for Southern Baptists. Clay L. Price and Phillip B. Jones, in a study made of 1976 SBC statistics, have demonstrated conclusively that new churches do a more effective job in evangelism.[13]

The study included 94 percent of the churches and 90 percent of the total baptisms in 1976. Only churches sponsoring daughter churches (missions) and those with inadequate statistics were omitted.

I have included some of the tables that reveal their findings. Let's see what they discovered.

Table 1 shows the number of baptisms by age of church.

1. One-third of SBC churches have been started since World War II.

2. The number of churches organized has been declining for the past thirty years.

1947-56   4,646
1957-66   3,796
1967-76   2,356

TABLE 1. **Number of Baptisms in 1976 by Age of Church**

Years	Number of Baptisms	Percent of Baptisms	Number of Churches	Percent of Churches
Less than 11	26,142	7.6	2,356	7.1
11-20	51,822	15.1	3,796	11.5
21-30	61,200	17.8	4,646	14.1
31-40	27,671	8.0	2,305	7.0
40+	177,322	51.5	19,867	60.3
Total	344,157	100.0	32,970	100.0

About one-half as many churches were organized between 1967-76 as between 1947-56.

3. This is a dangerous pattern in a nation with increasing numbers of unchurched and increasing numbers of ethnic and racial people-groups.

Table 2 shows the 1976 baptismal rate per 100 resident members by age and size of church.

1. Generally, the smaller the church, the higher the baptism rate. However, churches with more than 3,000 members are more evangelistically effective than churches with 500-2,999 members.

2. When examining the categories of church age, the younger the church, the higher the baptism rate. The baptism rate increases dramatically from older to younger churches:

A   *over 40 years old—3.7 per one hundred*
B   *31-40 years old—4.6 per one hundred*
C   *21-30 years old—5.7 per one hundred*
D   *11-20 years old—6.3 per one hundred*
E   *less than 11 years old—9.5 per one hundred.*

What did Price and Jones conclude from all this?

1. In Southern Baptist life the younger the church and the smaller the church, the higher the baptism rate.

2. Although the older churches had a lower baptism rate, because of sheer numbers, they had most of the baptisms. But if no churches had been organized in the years 1967-76, we would have baptized only 318,000 instead of 344,000 in 1976.

3. Since most of our baptisms come from churches that have been organized more than ten years, a major priority must be to increase the evangelistic effectiveness of all our churches. This must not be neglected.

4. Even though churches under eleven years of age only accounted for 10 percent of the baptisms, they were the most effective of all our churches in evangelism. Price and Jones concluded, "Thus, one of the key

TABLE 2. 1976 Baptism Rate by 1976 Resident Membership by Age of Church

Age of Church	Number of Resident Members													Total
	1-49	50-99	100-149	150-199	200-299	300-399	400-499	500-749	750-999	1000-1499	1500-1999	2000-2999	3000+	
Less than 11	11.4	10.2	8.9	8.0	7.9	7.3	6.6	6.1	5.7	7.1	7.8	—	—	9.5-E
11-20	7.1	7.6	6.3	6.4	5.9	5.4	5.0	4.7	5.1	5.6	4.8	5.3	2.6	6.3-D
21-30	7.8	5.7	5.5	5.3	4.9	4.7	4.4	4.1	4.2	3.8	4.8	4.7	3.6	5.7-C
31-40	5.5	5.4	4.8	4.5	4.2	4.4	3.9	3.7	3.2	3.4	3.4	2.2	6.4	4.6-B
40+	3.3	4.1	4.1	3.8	3.7	3.5	3.2	3.0	2.9	2.9	2.9	3.6	3.5	3.7-A
Total	5.5	5.4	4.9	4.6	4.5	4.2	3.8	3.5	3.4	3.4	3.4	3.8	4.0	4.7

reasons for establishing new churches is simply that
they are very effective in reaching people for Christ.
In fact, one way in which older churches might
increase their evangelistic effectiveness is through
mission outreach."[14]

What is my point? Both biblical example and modern
experience tell us that effective evangelism in a mobile
and plural society is essentially related to the
multiplication of churches in all the surging, changing
segments of that society. We will never be through with
church planting in our cities as long as new peoples
continue to come in and as long as there is geographical
and social mobility up and down the population. Church
planting is necessary to effective evangelism in the
modern American city.

III

This brings me to the third question: Since there is an
essential relationship between church planting and
effective evangelism, what does the need for new churches
require of us? Let me make seven suggestions.

1. *It requires that metropolitan churches develop
pluralistic strategies for a pluralistic world.*

In 1976 Andrew Greeley wrote a seminal article that
explored the inadequacies of the "melting pot" and
"mosaic" models for describing American ethnicity.[15] It is
obvious that America is not a melting pot. It is also
obvious that no one in America *has* to remain an ethnic, in
theory, at least, and often in actuality. One can choose to
identify with an ethnic community if he wants, but he
can't be forced morally or legally to do so.

Attempting to respond to this reality, Greeley observed
that there are at least four classifications of ethnics
within each group. The first can be called a nuclear
ethnic — someone who is explicitly and self-consciously
identified with ethnic values and heritage. His ethnic
identity is of controlling importance in most areas of his
life.

Second are the fellow-traveler ethnics, for whom

ethnicity is a relatively but not absolutely important part of their self-conscious identity.

A third classification of ethnic affiliation is the marginal ethnic. This person occasionally thinks of himself as an ethnic, but ethnicity is not normally crucial to his personal identity.

Finally, there are those who can be called assimilated ethnics.[16] These have alienated themselves from identification with their ethnic background. They have rejected ethnic values and heritage for assimilation with another culture.

Daniel Sanchez has used this concept in devising a five-year plan for evangelism in the state of New York as evangelism relates to ethnic groups. What Greeley has described as being true of ethnics, however, is true of every significant people-group in America, whether defined by ethnicity, race, socio-economic conditions, geographical sectionalism, or level of education. In fact, Greeley intended the concept to apply to all such groups, since he defines ethnicity as "religious, racial, nationality, linguistic, and geographical diversity in American society."[17] The number of people in each group is determined by different factors. The proportion of each of these classifications will differ within each group.

Most human characteristics can be described by Frederich Gauss' bell-shaped graph. The variations in ethnic self-consciousness within each group is not an exception to this principle. Using a display, we can show something of the pluralism present in most metropolitan communities in America and a way existing churches in those communities can respond to this pluralism. (See Figure 1.) At the same time we can take the teeth out of the objections to the homogeneous-unit principle that are often expressed today.

Assume that an upper-middle class, English-speaking, white church with a prestigious history finds itself in a rapidly changing community. When it finally comes to itself, it finds there are six significant people-groups living in its community. Thirty percent of the population consists of lower-middle class blacks who have fled the

FIGURE 1. **A Pluralistic Strategy for a Pluralistic World**

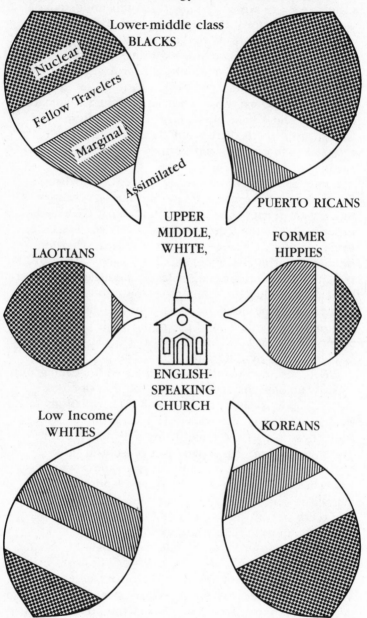

ghettos and moved to the area to better themselves. A large group of Puerto Ricans live in one distinct section of the community. A community of low-income whites, primarily from West Virginia, comprise 25 percent of the population. A small group of Laotians, a somewhat larger group of Koreans, and a community of former hippies who harbor drug traffic and have a distinctively libertine life style also live in the community.

How should this church address this community? It demands a pluralistic strategy. The church can realistically hope to reach those within each group who can be classified as assimilated. It should set out through regular channels of evangelism and ministry to do that. Everyone from each people-group who can be won to Christ and assimilated into the existing church should be aggressively evangelized.

With minor adaptation and flexibility, the existing church can probably reach many of those who are classified as marginals in each group. It might take a somewhat different style of worship or a black or Puerto Rican staff member, for example, to effectively penetrate this portion of each people-group.

However, for the fellow-traveler and the nuclear members of a people-group, an entirely different strategy is required. To reach them in significant numbers, new congregations—in homes, in storefronts, and small, simple buildings—will be essential. These people will not heed the gospel message if they do not hear it from their peers. They will not become responsible church members with people with whom they are culturally uncomfortable.

This approach to developing a pluralistic strategy can be taken by any church—white, black, or Spanish—in any kind of metropolitan community. I believe it provides a key for taking the pluralism of our world seriously.

In the plural world of our cities, only a plural strategy will suffice. That plural strategy, in my judgment, must include church planting. The communities of the city must be congregationalized, or re-congregationalized, with churches indigenous to the significant people-groups who are living there and who will move in tomorrow.

2. The need for thousands of new churches in urban areas for the purpose of effective evangelism requires *that we magnify the apostolic or church planting role along with our emphasis on the role of the pastor-teacher and the evangelist.* I have already spoken extensively about this, but I must stress it again. Winning America to Christ waits on thousands of new congregations. Thousands of new congregations wait on God-called, spirit-gifted, effectively trained, Christ-loving men and women who will spend their lives gathering new churches.

This means, of course, that we must alter our image of success and our system of rewards for pastors. Those called to the apostolic office must be recognized as significant members of the total task force for urban evangelization. The church planting role must be magnified so that our most able young people will give themselves to this task.

3. The needs that we have described *require a significant attitude change in reference to the size of churches. We must be willing to affirm and strengthen small churches.*

Please do not misunderstand me. I have said so much about small churches that many will feel that I oppose large churches. It is quite the contrary. I believe the day of the mega-church is just dawning. There will be a growing recognition, however, that huge churches are in reality a collection of smaller churches. In Latin America and Korea the largest churches in human history have been formed by multiplying house churches in great cities. This has been done with well trained lay pastors. This pattern can be followed in our cities.

Lyle Schaller calls the super churches of today "mini-denominations."[18] He is correct. The largest and most influential churches of the Southern Baptist Convention have yet to be planted. I believe that God will raise up innovative leaders among us who will develop huge congregations in *all* of the great cities of America through the multiplication of lay-led house churches whose leaders are bivocational. If Southern Baptist leaders will not respond, God will do it through others.

Quite apart from this, however, there needs to be an affirmation of small churches. We will always have small churches because we will always have churches in the midst of small people-groups, even in large cities. Some churches will have to be small to evangelize small people-groups adequately.

The fact that all churches are small when they are first planted is the primary reason that a positive attitude toward small churches is required of us. If we are faithful to God in evangelizing our modern cities, we must plant thousands of new churches. Newly planted churches are always small. The mean membership of all SBC churches started between 1967-76 was ninety-three in 1976.[19] We should not expect it to be any different with the thousands of churches we plant during the rest of this century.

4. The need to congregationalize and evangelize our cities requires us *to give special attention to training both laity and clergy in skills essential to these tasks in our cities.*

It is obvious from what I have said above that seminary-trained, ordained pastors will not be sufficient for the job ahead. The laity must be mobilized to the task, and men and women called of God but without the benefit of formal training must be utilized for church planting in our cities. I am convinced that as we are obedient to God in what he wants us to do in our cities, men will be raised up within existing churches to do this job.

Our seminaries have all moved toward training students in church planting skills. These programs need to be enlarged and developed. We need as extensive a curriculum in our seminaries for training in church extension as we have for evangelism.

But that is just the first step. A training program for lay leaders and bivocational church planters without formal education must be developed and implemented. Many lay

couples, like Aquila and Priscilla of old, have the
apostolic gift. They can gather new churches wherever
they live. Training programs for these must be devised
and implemented.

That is one kind of training, but the character of our
cities also requires that we *give major attention to
training church members in relational evangelism.*
Only such evangelism will be ultimately effective in our
cities. Wayne McDill has said it well: "Evangelism will
be effective toward making disciples in direct proportion
to its dependence on the establishment and cultivation
of meaningful relationships."[20]

The gospel always travels along the lines of human
relationship. Diametrically opposed to that principle, most
of our personal-witness training has been focused (1) on
casual or planned contacts with people we may never
have seen before and may never see again and (2) on
those people who are conceptually and emotionally ready
to receive Christ.

We have provided very little training for witnessing to
family members, work and school associates, next-door
neighbors, or members of our fraternal or civic
organizations. Yet these people make up most of our
world.[21] (See Figure 2.)

FIGURE 2. **My Oikos (Household): A Major Part of My World**

Anonymity is a way of life in urban America.[22] Our metropolitan areas have an impersonal life style. The sense of community is largely unknown. Closest relationships are family, work associates, and members of the various special interest groups to which people attach themselves. Developing ways of witnessing effectively in these continuing relationships is of crucial importance to effective congregationalizing and evangelizing in the city. The gospel usually travels from *oikos* to *oikos,* and these primary associations make up our "households." We must learn the way to make disciples out to the edge of our households and the procedure necessary to penetrate other households with the good news of Christ.

The second feature typical of our evangelism training has been its focus on people ready to make decisions. This kind of training is built on several assumptions— first, that the person to whom we bear witness is aware that there is one supreme God; next, that the person has sufficient knowledge of Christianity. We also assume that the person has a grasp of the implications of the gospel and has a general positive attitude toward Jesus Christ.

Those are rash assumptions in the face of the pluralism of our cities. Evangelism training must prepare us to recognize the level of awareness present in each individual and equip us to give the kind of witness needed at each level. Although many are familiar with James Engel's evangelism scale (see Figure 3), we need to study it and incorporate it into our witness-training efforts. Ralph Neighbour has developed an equally helpful tool in his *Touch Ministry Basic Training Manual.* (See Figure 4.) Called the "Awareness Pyramid," it graphically pictures the way people come to Christ from "unawareness" to "commitment." It includes a method for taking the new Christian toward "characterization" which we know as the *Survival Kit.*

Touch Ministry training includes an intensive effort to train people to recognize the levels of awareness in reference to the claims of Christ and to share Christ with them in a manner appropriate to their understanding.

FIGURE 3. Engel's Evangelistic "Countdown"

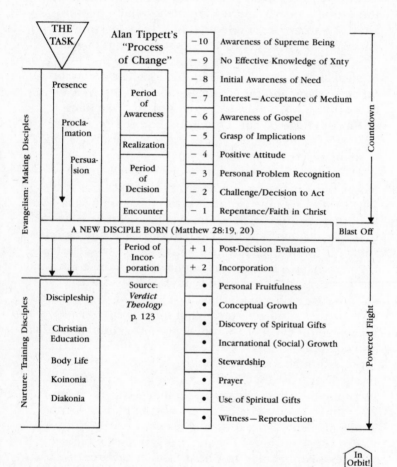

THE TASK	Alan Tippett's "Process of Change"		
		− 10	Awareness of Supreme Being
	Period of Awareness	− 9	No Effective Knowledge of Xnty
Presence		− 8	Initial Awareness of Need
Procla-mation		− 7	Interest — Acceptance of Medium
		− 6	Awareness of Gospel
	Realization	− 5	Grasp of Implications
Persua-sion	Period of Decision	− 4	Positive Attitude
		− 3	Personal Problem Recognition
		− 2	Challenge/Decision to Act
	Encounter	− 1	Repentance/Faith in Christ
A NEW DISCIPLE BORN (Matthew 28:19, 20)			Blast Off
	Period of Incor-poration	+ 1	Post-Decision Evaluation
		+ 2	Incorporation
Discipleship	Source: *Verdict Theology* p. 123	•	Personal Fruitfulness
		•	Conceptual Growth
Christian Education		•	Discovery of Spiritual Gifts
		•	Incarnational (Social) Growth
Body Life		•	Stewardship
Koinonia		•	Prayer
Diakonia		•	Use of Spiritual Gifts
		•	Witness — Reproduction

Evangelism: Making Disciples

Nurture: Training Disciples

Countdown

Powered Flight

In Orbit!

Source: *Your Church and Church Growth,* C. Peter Wagner, 1976

FIGURE 4. **The Way People Come to Christ . . .**

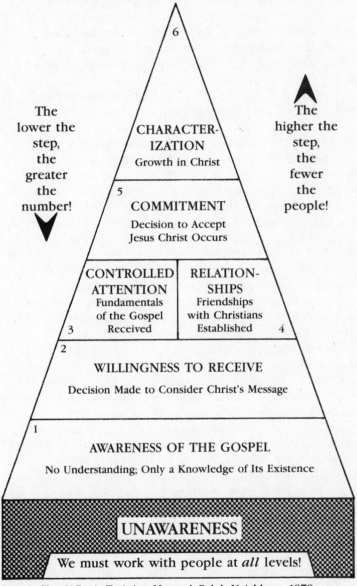

The lower the step, the greater the number! ∨

The higher the step, the fewer the people!

6

5 CHARACTER-IZATION
Growth in Christ

COMMITMENT
Decision to Accept Jesus Christ Occurs

3 CONTROLLED ATTENTION
Fundamentals of the Gospel Received

RELATION-SHIPS
Friendships with Christians Established 4

2 WILLINGNESS TO RECEIVE
Decision Made to Consider Christ's Message

1 AWARENESS OF THE GOSPEL
No Understanding; Only a Knowledge of Its Existence

UNAWARENESS
We must work with people at *all* levels!

Source: *Touch Basic Training Manual,* Ralph Neighbour, 1979

It is clear that an effective witness with someone who is a "−10" or completely unaware of the gospel requires a longer, more intensive, life-giving relationship than working with someone who has grown up in an evangelical church and who, when you meet him, is deeply aware that he needs his sins forgiven.

The urban life style demands workers thoroughly trained in relational evangelism and church planting skills.

5. The need to congregationalize and evangelize in our cities requires *that we pray much.* I do not believe we will see thousands of new churches planted in every city among every stratum of our society until we ask the Father for them. I am not talking about prayer as usual. I'm talking about the persistent, united prayer that has led to spiritual awakening in other ages. I'm talking about the kind of prayer that has gone on for twenty-five years in Korea. Now thousands are coming to Christ there every week. Our cities will never be evangelized nor congregationalized without a spiritual awakening that will not only bring churches to life but also will create a hunger for God in the general community.

We must begin to seek God's face with all our hearts if we would see American cities come to Christ.

6. The need to church all peoples and places in our cities adequately requires *that churches plan congregational strategies cooperatively and that they give serious consideration to the activity of other denominational groups.* There is a significant need for an overall strategy for each total metropolitan area. However, such strategies should, in my opinion, affirm the autonomy and mission of local congregations and not bind one denominational group by the strategy restrictions of another. Such restrictions could hinder the multiplication of churches where they are needed or hinder the growth of existing churches.

7. The task before us requires *that we march out boldly toward the goal.* What we have been achieving is abysmally inadequate. We need a new appreciation of the Lordship of Christ and a new image of ourselves as his

servants. We read his words, "All authority is given to me in heaven and on earth," but we seldom appropriate that authority. Our innermost self often says "no authority has been given to him, at least on earth." I remind you, however, that he is Lord! He is Lord of the Church and Lord of the universe. He is Lord of the city. He has authority over secularism and pluralism just as he has authority over disease and death. The modern city is no problem to him. It is a problem to us because we have not recognized his supreme authority and submitted to it totally. Our problem with evangelizing the city is essentially a spiritual problem.

Jesus is Lord, and he has all authority. This world is his. The Father has given it to him (Psalm 2). Satan, the prince of this world has been judged! Some insist that "principalities and powers" in the New Testament refers to demonic powers. Others say the terms refer to the authority structures of human society. Whichever interpretation you choose, Jesus is the head over *all* authorities and powers. Paul says that he (Christ) has disarmed them, triumphing over them (Col. 2:15). Jesus is Lord. America is his. The city is his! He has many people in every city!

What does this mean? It means we can proclaim the gospel with confidence that some will hear. We can evangelize without fear. We can anticipate that churches will be planted. It means that we can plan, dare, try, and expect to achieve. It means we can be bold in our obedience.

The need for planting new churches as bases for effective evangelism in our cities requires this kind of faith and this kind of effort.

NOTES

[1]*The Quarterly Review,* Vol. 40, No. 4, July-Sept., 1980, p. 77.
[2]I follow Donald A. McGavran, "Church Growth in America through Planting New Churches," an unpublished paper, 1976, in this section. See "Reaching People Through New Congregations," in Donald McGavran and George G. Hunter III, *Church Growth Strategies That*

Work (Nashville: Abingdon Press, 1980), pp. 99-120. This is a revision and enlargement of the earlier article.

[3]This imprecise estimate and those that follow were arrived at by saying:

(a) 65 percent Americans are church members = 146.25 million rounded to 145 million
(b) 35 percent not Christians = 78.5 million rounded to 80 million
(c) 3 out of 5 Christians are inactive = 87.5 million rounded to 90 million

[4]McGavran, *op. cit.,* p. 2.

[5]C. Kirk Hadaway, "A Compilation of Southern Baptist Churches and Resident Members Located in Standard Metropolitan Statistical Areas, 1978," research document published by Home Mission Board, SBC, Atlanta, GA, 1979, pp. 6, 24.

[6]PRRC *Emerging Trends,* Vol. 1, No. 6, June, 1979.

[7]Andrew M. Greeley, "Catholics Prosper While the Church Crumbles," *Psychology Today,* 1976, p. 44.

[8]Oscar I. Romo, "America's Ethnicity," in Language Missions Department, HMB, *America's Ethnicity* (Atlanta: Home Mission Board, SBC, 1978), n.p.

[9]*Newsweek,* July 7, 1980, p. 27.

[10]Language Missions Department, *America's Ethnicity,* n.d. I have followed this document in all the statistics that follow.

[11]Arthur F. Glasser, "Liberation Is In, the Unreached Out in Melbourne's View of the Kingdom," *Christianity Today,* June 27, 1980, p. 50.

[12]Lyle E. Schaller, "Why Start New Churches?" *The Circuit Rider,* May, 1979, p. 3.

[13]Clay L. Price and Phillip B. Jones, "A Study of the Relationship of Church Size and Church Age to Number of Baptisms and Baptism Rate," Atlanta: Department of Church Extension, HMB, SBC, May, 1978. I have followed this study closely in this section.

[14]*Ibid.,* p. 9.

[15]Andrew Greeley, "Is Ethnicity Unamerican?" *New Catholic World,* pp. 106-112.

[16]Greeley actually calls these "alienated" ethnics, describing them from the point of view of the people-group. I follow Daniel R. Sanchez, "A Five Year Plan of Growth for the Ministry of the Baptist Convention of New York in the Area of Evangelism," D. Min. dissertation, Fuller Theological Seminary, Pasadena, CA, pp. 242-247, in calling these "assimilated," describing them from the viewpoint of the existing church.

[17]Greeley, "Is Ethnicity Unamerican?" p. 106.

[18]Quoted in Jere Allen and George W. Bullard, Jr., *Hope for the Church in the Changing Community* (mimeographed book; Atlanta: Home Mission Board, SBC, 1980), p. 25.

19Price and Jones, *op. cit.,* p. 5.

20Wayne McDill, *Making Friends for Christ* (Nashville: Broadman Press, 1979), p. 6.

21Oscar Thompson, professor of evangelism at SWBTS, has performed a significant ministry for Southern Baptists by calling attention to these circles of relationship and the way they describe our world.

22See Francis M. DuBose, *How Churches Grow in an Urban World* (Nashville: Broadman Press, 1978), pp. 112 ff.

4. *Take time to create a climate for church planting in your congregation.* I want to put the emphasis on *take time.* The next chapter will go into some detail about ways this can be done. However, I want to make one point here: A congregational strategy for church planting will not be born overnight.

5. *Do not cling to traditional methods, no matter how "sanctified" they are, if they do not work.* Major on effectiveness, not on efficiency. An effective congregational strategy for church planting demands flexibility.

6. *Study principles and procedures of church planting yourself, and train your laity in those principles.* Your key church planting families should be raised up out of your own church.

7. *Plan to stay long enough in the church where you are serving – or where you go to serve – to see the strategy through to the end.* A congregational strategy for church planting demands years — not months — of commitment.

I believe that church planting is very closely related to the apostolic gift. I fervently and regularly pray not only for Southern Baptists, but for all Christians — that God will raise up apostles, gifted men and women, who can gather churches. We desperately need them today in America.

NOTES

[1]Jack Redford, *Planting New Churches* (Nashville: Broadman Press, 1979), pp. 22, 23.
[2]See William A. Lumpkin, *Baptist Foundations in the South* (Nashville: Broadman Press, 1961), for the full story of this remarkable church.
[3]Though he does not stress mega-churches, Peter Wagner has said that one vital sign of a healthy church is that it is "big enough." By "big enough" he meant large enough for the functioning of its own philosophy of ministry and for extension growth. See *Your Church Can Grow* (Glendale, CA: Regal Books, 1976), pp. 84, 93.
[4]Clay Price and Phillip Jones, "A Study of the Relationship of Church Size and Church Age to Number of Baptisms and Baptism Rates" (mimeographed document, prepared for Department of Church Extension, Home Mission Board, Southern Baptist Convention, Atlanta, GA, 1978).